HEALTH PLANS
UNM

T0094083

HEALTH PLANS UNMASKED

A Physician's Guide to Working
with Health Insurers

MARTIN LUSTICK, MD

JOHNS HOPKINS UNIVERSITY PRESS
Baltimore

Johns Hopkins University Press
2715 North Charles Street
Baltimore, Maryland 21218
www.press.jhu.edu

Library of Congress Cataloging-in-Publication data is available.

ISBN 978-1-4214-4676-9 (paperback)
ISBN 978-1-4214-4677-6 (ebook)

A catalog record for this book is available from the British Library.

*Special discounts are available for bulk purchases of this book. For more information,
please contact Special Sales at specialsales@jh.edu.*

To my best friend and soul mate—my wife, Karen

CONTENTS

PREFACE

It's been 55 years since I returned from a semester abroad in my junior year of college and decided I wanted to pursue a career in medicine. As a history major, this represented a sudden and dramatic shift in focus for me, but it began a fascinating journey through the maze of modern health care. After completing my pediatric residency at Children's Hospital National Medical Center in Washington, DC, I began a 17-year stint with Kaiser Permanente in the capital area. In addition to a busy pediatric practice, I gradually took on various management roles, culminating in my final 6 years as chief operating officer for the medical group, which at that point had 800 physicians, 200 advance practice providers, and more than 500,000 capitated lives under our care.

After leaving KP, I spent 2 years as the chief medical officer of ThompsonHealth, a small health system in the Finger Lakes region of western New York. For the next 13 years, I served as the CMO of Excellus BCBS, the Blue Cross plan in upstate New York. In that role I had the privilege of helping lead efforts to pursue value-based care with providers across the state and to learn about the labyrinth of infrastructure, functions, and culture that underlies the behavior of health insurance companies across the country.

In January 2020, just before the pandemic hit the United States, I joined my colleagues Dr. Betty Rabinowitz, Graham Brown, and Chris Emper to form the advisors team at NextGen Healthcare. Combining our accumulated experience and knowledge, we have dedicated ourselves to helping provider organizations successfully navigate the treacherous path from volume to value.

For all of the provider groups that are struggling to improve care and outcomes for the individuals and communities they serve, this book is for you.

ACKNOWLEDGMENTS

I have been the fortunate recipient of intellectual and emotional generosity throughout my career. I extend my gratitude to the physicians and staff of Kaiser Permanente and ThompsonHealth, to my health plan colleagues across the country, and to health care providers and leaders across upstate New York. Thank you for sharing your knowledge and experience over the past 35 years. A special thanks to Dr. Betty Rabinowitz, who brought me in to NextGen Healthcare, encouraged me to write this book, and has been a mentor, colleague, and friend. Likewise, Graham Brown, my other partner at NextGen, listened to my concerns, offered sage advice, and was always supportive. He also provided invaluable background information on payviders. Chris Emper graciously shared his expertise regarding regulatory issues, and Spencer Beck read and edited the first draft of the manuscript. Finally, my brother, Ian Lustick, gave me important feedback, advice, and support that made publication of this book possible.

PART I

The Basics

CHAPTER 1

Historical Context

Forty-six hundred years ago in ancient Egypt, Imhotep described the diagnosis and treatment of 200 diseases. Twenty-one hundred years later, Alcmaeon of Croton (an ancient Greek colony on the Italian peninsula) first distinguished arteries from veins. More than 1,400 years then passed before Rhazes first identified smallpox in Persia, and almost 900 years after that, in 1796, Edward Jenner developed the smallpox vaccine. Another century passed when, in 1895, Wilhelm Roentgen discovered X-rays. The year 1922 saw insulin used for the first time to treat diabetes, and in 1928 Sir Alexander Fleming discovered penicillin.[1]

It took 4,500 years to go from the first recorded description of 200 disease states to the beginnings of modern medicine with X-rays, insulin, and penicillin. Then, in just one century, we created antibiotics for virtually every bacterial pathogen, and antivirals to treat HIV and to cure hepatitis C. We developed ultrasound, CAT scans, PET scans, and MRIs to view structures and functions throughout the body. And we invented neutron beam radiation, genomic vaccines, and robotic surgery for cancer. In

2020, we developed a vaccine for a brand-new virus, SARS-CoV-2, to protect against COVID-19 in less than a year. We can now treat heart attacks with stent placement and strokes with clot-busting drugs. Computers have become central to medicine from having digitally enhanced medical devices such as continuous glucose monitors, pacemakers, and robotics to electronic health records, population health platforms, health-data exchanges, and virtual visits.

The pace of change in medical diagnosis and treatment has been so rapid that the only way to keep up has been to subspecialize, leaving clinicians with ever-narrowing silos of expertise. We now have oncologists who spend their entire career focused on one type of cancer, orthopedic surgeons who specialize in a single joint, cardiac surgeons who specialize in a single valve, and so it goes.

As specialization accelerates, so too does complexity for the patients. People fit into these highly specialized silos only for short periods of time or for limited portions of their overall health status. Unfortunately, it has become increasingly difficult to find anyone involved in the care journey who ensures that a patient's overall health care needs are met by the variety of specialists they encounter. The United States faces an increasing shortage of primary care providers, even as those who remain are overwhelmed by the demand for their services combined with the ever-increasing complexity of their practices.

The financial implications of this continually accelerating pace of change have been profound. Health care costs have gone from 5% of GDP in 1960 to 18% in 2020. Consider the cost of prescription drugs. When Nexium was introduced in 2001 at $120 for a one-month supply, it was considered inordinately expensive. Just 12 years later, Sovaldi was introduced at $80,000 for a three-month course to cure hepatitis C. An even more dramatic example is Acthar gel, used to treat infantile spasms at a cost of $40 per vial in 2000, and the exact same drug costing $40,000 per vial in 2018. These dramatic escalations in cost have driven insurance companies, employers, and the government to seek creative responses. They have propelled a rapid migration to high-deductible plans with greater consumer cost sharing, more focus on utilization management programs, and, most recently, attention toward alternative payment methods with providers.

A lack of appreciation for payment and financing complexity has led many both within and outside of health care to point to health insurers as an evil force. Health plans can be viewed cynically as only caring about money, yet a similar cynical conclusion could be drawn about today's providers. Some of them make huge profits by owning equipment that is used for expensive tests or procedures that their specialty requires, or they have ownership interest in the facilities where their specialty services are provided. These capital-intensive investments create enormous financial pressure on their owners to use the equipment. Just as it is overly simplistic and disparaging to draw this conclusion about providers, so too is the tendency to paint health insurers as "the bad guys."

This book is intended to support a deeper understanding of the payer role in the health care ecosystem—to look clearly at "the man behind the curtain." It is written for leaders of provider organizations who seek answers to their questions and concerns about how they can get paid just to take good care of their patients. They want to know, Why do I not get my fair share of rising health care premiums? Why do I see so many delays and incorrect payments from insurance companies? Why are coverage and payment issues so complicated and variable? How do I position my practice to get ahead of the curve?

This endeavor is not for the faint of heart, as it is akin to sorting a plate of spaghetti. Taken in its entirety, the book provides the reader with an understanding of the capabilities, limitations, strategies, and vulnerabilities of health plans in the current, complex world of the US health care system. More importantly, it provides a foundation that can be leveraged to build stronger relationships with payers that ensure a sustainable path to value-based care.

The chapters are structured to provide insight into specific aspects of the payer world. At the end of each chapter, the reader will find a short list of insights and takeaways for further consideration. Again, the goal is to help providers improve their ability to chart a successful course toward an uncertain future. Just like good clinical care, success on the business side of health care comes from expanding our knowledge base and applying diligence and strong values to every endeavor.

CHAPTER 2

What Is a Health Plan?

When providers talk about health plans, health insurance, and managed care organizations (MCOs), they often use the three terms interchangeably. In fact, these terms have different meanings that hold important implications for providers and, ultimately, for all of us. "Health plan" is a generic term that refers to any organization that provides coverage for health care expenses. Examination of the historical context will elucidate the important distinctions between an insurance company and an MCO. An appreciation of the historical arc of third-party payers in health care will give providers a good foundation for understanding the complex set of challenges and opportunities they face today.

Health insurance took hold in the United States as a result of wage freezes imposed during World War II. Employers found that they could attract workers by offering health insurance as a benefit, and the government made this easy by agreeing not to tax it as income. Blue Cross and Blue Shield were the first to provide indemnity-based health insurance. Similar in concept to car insurance, in return for a monthly premium the subscriber was reimbursed for their financial losses related to a covered service, that is, they were indemnified. That reimbursement was either a set amount or a percentage of charges. For a decade or more after World War II, commercial health insurance grew and became a standard for a large percentage of the population.[1] From 1940 to 1950, the insured population in the United States grew from less than 20 million to more than 60 million and by 1960, to almost 140 million. In other words, in 1940 only 15% of the US population had health insurance and by 1960 it was close to 80%. Because health insurance was almost exclusively offered as an employment benefit, it was the poor and elderly who were left without coverage. So, in 1965, with the passage of the Medicare and Medicaid Act, the hope was that these federal government programs would fill the gap in coverage and ensure that all Americans had access to affordable care.

Prior to the Health Maintenance Organization (HMO) Act of 1973, indemnity insurance was the predominant form of coverage for most Americans. Under that model, the transactions were all between the insurance company and the patient. There was no provider network and therefore no contract between the insurance company and the provider. Patients saw whomever they chose, paid the provider directly, and submitted a claim for reimbursement.

The HMO Act of 1973 forced employers with more than 25 employees, who offered health benefits, to offer HMO coverage to their employees.[2] It also created financial incentives for health insurers to become MCOs. The result was rapid expansion of HMOs over the next 20 years. While the HMO Act essentially expired in 1995, its overwhelming impact persists to this day. In becoming MCOs, insurance companies had undergone a transformation. They were suddenly responsible for establishing a network of providers, both physicians and hospitals that contractually agreed to care for the members of the health plan. Patients would receive care from those providers, but claims would be paid directly by the health plan to the provider—no more indemnification of the patient. Unlike insurance companies that function as financial intermediaries, MCOs sell a network of providers and services to their customers. As a result, they are at risk for issues such as access and quality of care.

With the advent of managed care, health plans suddenly needed a clinical team for credentialing, quality oversight, and cost control, thus converting them into MCOs. In today's world, MCOs administer a variety of managed care products such as HMO, point of service (POS), exclusive provider organization (EPO), and preferred provider organization (PPO). All of these are variations of health plan–contracted networks and services that are sold to beneficiaries with an implied health plan accountability for access, quality, and provider payments.

While many providers might prefer to go back to the "good old days" of indemnity insurance, that model had its drawbacks. Under indemnity coverage, insurance companies render denials *after* a service is provided if it is not covered by the policy. This could leave providers pursuing patients for payments for those services. Even if services are covered, many patients would not be able to afford to pay unless and until they receive payment from the insurer. As providers today often struggle to collect co-pays and deductibles, they would have significantly increased challenges with accounts receivable under a pure indemnity product.

With an understanding of how health insurers became MCOs, the next step is to explore the evolution of Medicare and Medicaid, and the expanding variety of commercial insurance products.

Providers will be well served to understand each of these lines of business as they navigate their relationships with payers.

Key Takeaways

1. Since the HMO Act of 1973, traditional indemnity insurance has all but disappeared.
2. The rise of managed care products forced insurers to get deeply involved with clinical issues in health care.

Recommendations

1. Ask health plan for breakdown of attributed membership by line of business and product line.
2. In commercial contracts, be sure to clarify which, if any, product lines are excluded.

CHAPTER 3

Medicare

With the passage of the Medicare and Medicaid Act in 1965, the federal government stepped directly into the health insurance market and forever altered the dynamics of how health care is financed. Medicare came into being at a time when policy makers saw that the elderly represented the single largest portion of the population that lacked health insurance. It was intended to supplement commercial insurance and reduce or eliminate the problem of the uninsured. It is therefore ironic that Medicare has evolved to become the foundation of benefit design, coverage determinations, and provider payments for commercial health insurance. When Medicare announces coverage of a new technology, for example, it is virtually inevitable that commercial insurers will follow suit. When Medicare began alternative payment programs, commercial insurers jumped on board and began creating their own versions of accountable care organizations (ACOs).

Medicare started with what today are known as Parts A and B. Part A covers hospitalization, subacute nursing facility care, hospice care, and some home health services. Generally, there is no premium for Part A and no co-pays. Deductibles in Part A are for each hospitalization and in 2022 were $1,556 per annum. Part B covers outpatient and professional services. Premiums for Part B were $3 per month in 1966 but have risen an average of 7.6% annually since then. In 2007, a sliding scale premium was introduced based on income so that in 2022 monthly premiums ranged from $170.10 for individuals earning less than $90,000 to $578.30 for those earning more than $500,000. Part B also includes a deductible of $233 for 2022.[1]

A lesser-known element of Medicare Parts A and B is that the federal government does not actually pay any claims. Since Medicare's inception in 1966, private health care insurers have processed medical claims for Medicare beneficiaries. Originally these entities were known as Part A fiscal intermediaries (FIs) and Part B carriers. In 2003, the Centers for Medicare and Medicaid Services (CMS) was directed to replace the Part A FIs and Part B carriers with A/B Medicare administrative contractors (MACs) in accordance with the Federal Acquisition Regulation (FAR).[2]

Parenthetically, since the beginning of Medicare, these contractors have been largely developed and maintained by Blue Cross plans. Table 3.1, showing the MACs for Medicare Parts A and B, is illustrative. All but one, the Wisconsin Physicians Service, are subsidiaries of a Blue Cross plan.[3]

Medicare Part C is more commonly referred to as Medicare Advantage. This serves as a substitute for Medicare Parts A and B (and sometimes D). Under Medicare Part C, commercial health plans receive a risk-adjusted and geographically adjusted monthly premium for each enrollee in their Medicare Advantage plan. The plans are required to provide coverage for all services covered in Parts A and B, and are allowed to cover additional benefits

Table 3.1. A/B Medicare administrative contractors

Medicare administrative contractor	Owner	Geography of jurisdiction
Noridian	BCBS North Dakota	West Coast, Rocky Mountain states, and HI and AK
Novitas and First Coast Service Options (FSCO)	Florida BCBS	South Central states plus FL, NJ, DL, MD, and PA
Palmetto, Celerian Group Customer Service	BCBS South Carolina	AL, GA, TN, SC, NC, VA, and WV
National Government Services (NGS)	Wellpoint/Anthem	WI, MN, IL, OH, and KY
Wisconsin Physicians Service (WPS)	Independent	MI, IN, IA, MO, NE, and KS

Source: A/B Jurisdiction Map, June 2021, https://www.cms.gov/files/document/ab-jurisdiction-map-jun-2021.pdf

including part D. Their planned benefit packages and premiums then must be submitted for review and approval by June 1 for implementation the following calendar year.

While earlier modifications to Medicare provided some prescription drug coverage for some beneficiaries, it wasn't until Medicare Part D was created in 2003 that this coverage became available to all Medicare recipients. This complex plan was then phased in over the next three years. In an effort to minimize the cost of the program and encourage individuals to be thoughtful about prescription drug usage, the plan was designed with a "donut hole." In the 2022 version, the beneficiary paid the first $445, had a co-pay or coinsurance depending on their plan for the next $3,995, and paid 25% of the cost for the next $2,620. At this point, the beneficiary reached "catastrophic coverage" with 5% coinsurance for the remainder of the year.[4] In the initial version, the third phase was the "donut hole," where the beneficiary paid 100% of the costs.

As if Medicare Parts A, B, C, and D aren't enough, there are also 10 more Medicare policies that relate to commercially sponsored supplemental or "Medigap" plans. In the same legislation that established Medicare Part D, the federal government required federal licensing of all Medicare supplemental plans offered by commercial insurers, creating a much more complex regulatory environment for these insurance products. In fact, because states continue to play a role in regulating these products, three states—Massachusetts, Wisconsin, and Minnesota—do not follow the federal categories, but have created their own. For the other 47 states, Medigap plans are divided into 10 categories labeled, A, B, C, D, F, G, K, L, M, and N (table 3.2); these 10 categories are in order of increasing level of benefits provided.[5]

Providers tend to notice two things about Medicare. First is that they tend to get reimbursed less for Medicare Part B recipients than they do by commercial payers. Historically, the other distinguishing feature of Medicare was that there were no prior authorization requirements, but that is changing. Under Medicare Part D, prior authorization is common, and in 2020 it was added as a requirement for a limited number of outpatient procedures.[6]

In addition to the evolving complexity of Medicare products and benefits, in the past decade CMS has aggressively pursued alternative payment models with providers. Providers who participate in Medicare Parts A and B are therefore likely to be familiar with meaningful use (MU), merit-based incentive payment system (MIPS), accountable care organizations (ACOs), alternative payment models (APMs), and ACO REACH (Realizing Equity, Access, and Community Health). All of these programs have in common an attempt to provide financial incentives to providers to transition away from paper, to improve quality, and to

Table 3.2. Medigap plans

| | | | | | Medigap plans | | | | | |
Medigap benefits	A	B	C	D	F	G	K	L	M	N
Part A coinsurance and hospital costs up to an additional 365 days after Medicare benefits are used up	Yes	Yes	Yes	Yes	Yes	Yes	Yes	Yes	Yes	Yes
Part B coinsurance or copayment	Yes	Yes	Yes	Yes	Yes	Yes	50%	75%	Yes	Yes
Blood (first 3 pints)	Yes	Yes	Yes	Yes	Yes	Yes	50%	75%	Yes	Yes
Part A hospice care coinsurance or copayment	Yes	Yes	Yes	Yes	Yes	Yes	50%	75%	Yes	Yes
Skilled nursing facility care coinsurance	No	No	Yes	Yes	Yes	Yes	50%	75%	Yes	Yes
Part A deductible	No	Yes	Yes	Yes	Yes	Yes	50%	75%	50%	Yes
Part B deductible	No	No	Yes	No	Yes	No	No	No	No	No
Part B excess charge	No	No	No	No	Yes	Yes	No	No	No	No
Foreign travel exchange (up to plan limits)	No	No	80%	80%	80%	80%	No	No	80%	80%
Out-of-pocket limit	N/A	N/A	N/A	N/A	N/A	N/A	$5,880 in 2020[a]	$2,940 in 2020[b]	N/A	N/A

Source: "How to Compare Medigap Policies," https://www.medicare.gov/supplements-other-insurance/how-to-compare-medigap-policies
[a] $6,220 in 2021
[b] $3,110 in 2021

reduce overall cost trends in health care. As will become clear in part IV regarding contracting, those key attributes have served as the foundation for the variety of APMs employed by commercial health plans, spanning their Medicare, Medicaid, and commercial lines of business.

As value-based arrangements become a larger component of a provider's contracting landscape, the complexity of Medicare rules for patients, health plans, and providers takes on material significance, impacting the sustainability of provider strategies. Before we delve more deeply into these issues, it's important to understand the evolution of Medicaid and commercial lines of business, as well as the basic provider-facing functions of commercial health insurers.

Key Takeaways
1. Medicare has a complex set of products.
2. Medicare impacts coverage and payment policies of commercial health plans.

Recommendations
1. Since different products within Medicare have different rules, ask health plan for distribution of attributed Medicare membership by product line.
2. Since Medigap products are not Part C, providers need to clarify with each health plan whether those members are being attributed.

CHAPTER 4

Medicaid

Although Medicaid's history is closely tied to Medicare, the two programs are quite different, and have been from the start. The legislation signed by President Lyndon B. Johnson in 1965 that established Medicare as a federal insurance program for anyone over 65 also created Medicaid as a state-run program, partially funded by the federal government, that was available only to those on public assistance. Unlike Medicare, states were free to choose if, and to a large extent how, they would participate.

The federal government would make payments to states to pay for half or more of their costs in furnishing services to beneficiaries. At the same time, the program was framed to give states considerable latitude in fashioning their medical assistance programs. States that elected to participate were required to furnish a core set of basic health services to public assistance recipients. They were also allowed to offer additional services at their option and could elect to serve "medically needy" individuals who did not receive public assistance. Then, as now, the Medicaid program combined federal mandates and state-selected options with respect to who receives services and what services are offered.

Over time both eligibility and benefit requirements have changed, but the ability of states to customize this program remains. To this day, states administer Medicaid programs and have flexibility to determine covered populations, covered services, health care delivery models, and methods for paying physicians and hospitals.

Even the Affordable Care Act of 2010 (ACA), which called for an expansion of Medicaid that standardized financial eligibility requirements, left significant control over the program to the states. The ACA's "expanded" Medicaid provided guaranteed coverage for anyone whose income was below the Federal Poverty Line—$12,760 for individuals. To minimize the burden on states, the ACA provided for the federal government to cover 100% of the additional cost initially, with phased reductions to 90% federal and 10% state cost sharing after 2020. The 2012 Supreme Court ruling, though, made Medicaid expansion voluntary, and as of February 2022, there were still 12 states, mostly in the Southeast, that had not adopted Medicaid expansion.

Even with continued significant variability across states, Medicaid has played an increasingly important role in financing health care services. Medicaid coverage accounts for nearly half of all births, 83% of poor children, 48% of children with special health care needs, and 45% of nonelderly adults with disabilities.[1] Medicaid enrollees in 2000 included 34.5 million individuals. As a result of Medicaid expansion included in the Affordable Care Act, this increased to 54.5 million in 2010 and reached 88.3 million as of April 2022. As a percentage of the insured population, Medicaid increased from 13.4% in 2008 to 26.6% in 2022.[2]

Given the long-term growth in Medicaid enrollment combined with continued variability across states, even providers with a minimal number of Medicaid patients would be well served to understand the details of their state's Medicaid programs. New York, for example, has programs for special populations such as those with HIV/AIDS or serious mental illness that provide extra benefits and funding to support the special needs of these populations. Well-positioned providers can align with these programs to augment care for their patients, even as they create new revenue opportunities for themselves.

Key Takeaways
1. Medicaid is highly variable from state to state.
2. One-quarter of the US population is covered by Medicaid.

Recommendations
1. Ask health plan for in-service on special membership categories in that state. Focus on revenue, benefit design, regulatory requirements, and quality measures.
2. Ask health plan to share overall quality scores and regulatory issues.
3. See summary recommendations in chapter 4.

CHAPTER 5

Commercial Insurance

Just as Medicare and Medicaid have grown more complex over time, so too have commercial insurance products. There are actually two separate layers of diversification within the commercial health insurance world. As mentioned in chapter 1, there is the basic benefit design, which has evolved from the original indemnity products to a wide variety of managed care products. Underneath this portfolio of network and benefit designs lies a set of funding and rating structures that further complicate the health care landscape. Even for providers that have not joined an independent physician association (IPA), are not in a clinically integrated network (CIN), and are not in a large multispecialty group, these layers of complexity significantly impact their practice from both a clinical and a business perspective.

Before the HMO Act of 1973, there were few health maintenance organizations (HMOs) in the country, with Kaiser Permanente being most notable among them. This was a model of coverage where consumers were offered a limited network of physicians and hospitals, often incorporating a "gatekeeper," with all care required to funnel through an assigned primary care provider (PCP). The first adjustment to this model was to create a point of service product, often referred to as HMO-POS or just POS. Essentially, this was the first "tiered network," where patients were allowed to go outside the narrow network defined by the HMO but had significantly increased cost sharing.

HMOs created complexity for providers by forcing them to customize their referral patterns to the providers that were in network, then further complicated it by adding POS and creating a greater dependency on the individual patient's ability and willingness to go "out of network." On top of that, because HMOs were the first managed care products, they introduced provider credentialing and prior authorization into the equation. The dissemination of the HMO model in the 1980s foreshadowed the nearly impenetrable complexity of today's health care. The combination of variable network design, authorization requirements, and patient cost sharing complicates the clinical management, workflow, and financial model of practices of all shapes and sizes.

As HMOs, even with POS, fell out of favor in the 1990s, health plans came up with less onerous products to add to their portfolio. Preferred provider organizations (PPOs) extended the POS concept by removing the requirement for a PCP, eliminating the gatekeeper role, and simply creating a tiered network with higher cost sharing for out-of-network services.

Exclusive provider organizations (EPOs) represented another variation on this theme. In EPOs patients can navigate without referrals as long as they stay within the network but have no out-of-network benefits. In today's world, outside of government programs, PPO is the predominant model, but most areas of the country do have some small portion of EPO, HMO, and POS as well.

With indemnity insurance still lingering in some parts of the country as well, providers experience the confusion and frustration of varying authorization rules, specialist availability, and patient financial burden. That variation starts within a single insurer and is then multiplied by the number of insurers with which the provider maintains contracts.

The unfortunate reality for providers is that within each of these product lines the range of funding mechanisms further multiplies these same challenges. Community rating provides the foundation of funding mechanisms in commercial insurance products. In this traditional approach to setting premiums for employers, health plan actuaries estimate the average predicted health care costs for everyone living within a given geographic area. In its simplest form, the health plan would divide the total estimated cost by the total number of people, then add a small administrative fee, and this would be the charged premium of an individual. In reality adjustments would be made to differentiate among individuals, couples, and families, but the principles are the same.

This approach reflects the traditional concept of any type of insurance. The idea is for everyone to chip in the same amount as a monthly premium, and thereby generate enough money to cover the costs of those who end up needing services. Insurance companies quickly learned that they could separate out groups into various levels of risk and adjust premiums accordingly. In health care, the simplest example is to charge higher premiums to smokers. The slippery slope here would lead insurers to block people with preexisting conditions in order to better control premiums, with the unfortunate consequence of ultimately only insuring people who least need coverage. The ACA established clear guidelines for insurers requiring that they employ an adjusted community-rating methodology.[1] Under these rules, health plans are limited to making adjustments based on age with a maximum ratio of 3:1 for the most expensive to least expensive premiums. Interestingly, they are also still allowed to charge extra for coverage of smokers. In general, policies offered on exchanges and those for small employers are community rated, but as employer size increases other approaches predominate.

Many employers observed that their employees were generally younger and healthier than the overall community, and they began to look for ways to avoid subsidizing the costs for the broader community. This was easiest for large employer groups. For example, a company with 5,000 employees might be providing coverage for 10,000 people. That's enough to make overall health care costs fairly predictable. If that group was generally younger and healthier than the community at large, employers could take the risk of covering those costs directly rather than "buying insurance"—hence the beginning of self-insured products.

It's worth noting that a significant consequence of this dynamic is an inevitable increase in premiums for community-rated products. As healthier, less expensive people are removed from the community risk pool, those left behind seeking individual or small group coverage are, in aggregate, higher risk. As a result, employer groups that were originally equivalent to the community risk pool gradually find themselves on the healthier end of the continuum. Those same groups would then be drawn toward self-insurance, placing continuous upward pressure on community-rated premiums.

In 1974, when the federal Employee Retirement Income Security Act (ERISA) was passed, it specifically shielded employers who self-insured their employees from state regulations.[2] That meant employers who chose self-insurance could benefit from having a lower risk pool than the community and, at the same time, modify benefits to reduce costs in ways that commercial insurers could not.

Even with this desire to self-insure, employers lacked the infrastructure to contract with providers and to process and pay claims, so they turned to insurers, and in some cases third-party administrators (TPAs), to fill that gap. In this instance, the employer pays the health plan (or TPA) a small monthly fee, and the health plan administers the benefits and pays providers based on the plan's contracted fee schedule. The employer then reimburses the health plan for all claims expenses. This type of arrangement is called an administrative services only (ASO) contract between the employer and the health plan or TPA.

TPAs are companies that either create a provider network or "rent" a provider network, and then focus purely on their ability to administer benefits and pay claims appropriately. Because they have no other health plan functions, like marketing, case management, or prior authorization, their fees are generally lower than what a health plan would charge. At the same time, TPAs often act as an intermediary, offering those other services to employer groups on an à la carte basis as "buy-up" programs. They contract for those specific services with vendors (sometimes a health plan) and mark up charges to employers as another source of profit.

For intermediate-sized employer groups or large groups averse to risk, experience-rated coverage offers a blend between traditional community-rated insurance and being self-insured. Employer groups with 500 to 1,000 employees make up the bulk of this category, but increasingly smaller groups are seeking this as well. Health plans take all the employers within a geographic area that seek experience-rated coverage and group them in a single risk pool. There are then two components to determining their annual change in premium. The individual prior experience of each group is taken together with the experience of the entire risk pool. The premium is then calculated with the weighting of these two estimates based on the size of each group. For the largest employers, their own experience weighs most heavily in the calculation, whereas for the smallest employers the experience of the entire risk pool predominates. Many employers view experience rating as a transition toward self-insurance. Because within a given year the employer pays premiums and the health plan pays all the claims, experience rating is considered a "fully insured" product, that is, the health plan, not the employer, carries the insurance risk. As a result, employers do not have the same flexibility to modify benefits that are possible with an ASO arrangement.

There is one other hybrid between ASO and fully insured worth mentioning: minimum premium.[3] In this arrangement, the plan and employer agree on a specific percentage of expected claims cost for which the employer will be responsible (usually 90%), and the health plan is at risk for all costs above that. This provides most of the tax benefits of being self-insured but limits risk for the employer.

In the last decade, yet another twist has been introduced into the funding design, and that is the dramatic increase in patient cost sharing with high-deductible health plans (HDHPs) and health savings accounts (HSAs). According to the Kaiser Family Foundation, enrollment in HDHPs rose from 4% of covered workers in 2006 to 28% in 2021.[4]

Even smaller employers have found that they can reduce health care costs but still maintain good coverage for their employees by introducing an HSA together with a high-deductible plan. They can buy a traditional insurance product from a health plan and include a significant deductible of perhaps $5,000. The employer can then fund their employees HSA for $4,500. The HDHP presents the employer with a lower premium and they also get tax relief for their contributions to the HSA.

From a provider perspective, the layering of multiple products, on multiple funding streams, with increasing financial risk for patients presents enormous challenges. Providers are forced to customize their treatment plans and business practices to each patient. Attempts to achieve efficiencies through standard operating procedures are undermined by the ever-increasing level of complexity related just to the financing of health care services.

In the next chapter, we will review the role of brokers and consultants as they further complicate things for providers, even as they attempt to simplify health care for their employer clients.

Key Takeaways
1. Today's commercial insurance represents a complex array of products, benefit designs, and funding arrangements.
2. These layers of complexity represent a root cause of provider frustrations.

Recommendations
1. Memberships among commercial products can significantly impact cost assumptions embedded in alternative payment models, so ask the health plan to explain its strategic approach to product line within their commercially insured population.

2. Summary of information requests from health plans (chapters 2, 3, 4):
   a. Distribution of attributed Medicare membership by product line.
   b. Trends in membership by product line across their commercial lines of business.

CHAPTER 6

Brokers and Consultants

In the realm of employer-based health care, brokers and consultants play a significant role that ultimately impacts the entire health care ecosystem. For small businesses that are community rated, brokers typically serve the function of connecting the business to a variety of vendors that manage their employee benefits. A single broker might arrange the health care, employee assistance program, life insurance, and disability coverage for these employers. Health plans view these brokers as an extension of their sales force. They are generally paid on commission and the health plan sales leaders will meet with them regularly to keep them up to date on the latest changes to products and benefits. Within a geographic region, health plans will compete on the amount and the way brokers are paid to maximize the likelihood that those brokers will recommend their plan to employers. Brokers generally have no leverage to influence benefit design, so the impact on providers is limited.

The term *consultant* is used here to refer to those organizations that support benefits management leaders in large employer groups, most of which are self-funded for health care. These consultants are generally paid by the employer group, not the health plan, and provide specialized, expert support to the employer when it comes to the specifics of their health care benefit design and their choice of vendors to supply those benefits. Because self-insurance frees employers from many of the regulatory requirements that restrict health plans, these consultants often propose creative benefit designs that maximize value for the particular employer. A consultant might observe that orthopedic costs are particularly high for an employer group and propose high co-pays for elective orthopedic surgeries, the requirement of a second opinion before covering these surgeries, or channeling employees to a lower-cost provider through customized network design. Consultants often have relationships with pharmacy benefit management (PBM) companies or care management organizations, and they will recommend these carve-outs to employer groups as alternatives to the health plan or TPA that administers the employer's benefits.

These customized solutions can create significant confusion for providers. Two patients with the same insurer and the same apparent benefit design may have completely different pharmacy formularies, prior authorization rules, or even in-network specialists. In some instances, the brokers may also specify whether and how an employer should include their employees in value-based arrangements. Health plans can refuse to accommodate some of these requests, but then they run the risk of losing that business to a competitor.

One of the many problems these customized approaches create is to drive complexity, and therefore errors, into the claims payment process. This is particularly problematic with health systems that self-insure their employees. It's not uncommon for a health system to create a tiered network so their employees receive maximum care within their delivery system. With a consultant designing this customized network, there is often a need to fill gaps in the system's geographic or specialty capabilities, so that the first tier of the network will include some "nonsystem" providers. The likelihood that a health plan will be able to seamlessly administer such a design is low. The result is often confusion and frustration for everyone involved: providers, patients, employers, and health plans.

With 60% of commercial insurance now self-funded, and with this segment continuing to grow, the complexity that consultants bring to health care should not be underestimated. While this creates obvious frustrations and challenges for providers, to those who are well positioned for value-based care, it also creates significant opportunities. Those opportunities are discussed further in chapter 9.

Key Takeaways
1. Consultants influence benefit and network design for self-insured employer groups.
2. Health plans have little control over this source of complexity and confusion for providers and patients.

Recommendations
1. Ask health plan to share distribution of attributed members under self-insured policies with customized, nonstandard benefit or network design.
2. Begin to build relationships with large local employers and their health care consultants.

PART II

Reimbursement Basics

CHAPTER 7

The ABCs of Fee-for-Service

Fee-for-service (FFS) contracts have served as the foundation of health care financing for decades. As early as 1966, the American Medical Association (AMA) created current procedural terminology (CPT) codes to enable consistent payment methodologies across the country. Despite the rise and fall of capitated independent physician association (IPA) agreements late in the twentieth century, and the ever-expanding array of alternative payment models in the past decade, most physician contracts still have FFS methodology at their core. Even as providers set their sights on a future that is defined by value-based payments, it remains critically important to understand the FFS world.

By the 1980s, the Centers for Medicare and Medicaid Services (CMS) experienced continuously escalating costs and significant variations in payments using their "usual, customary, and reasonable" methodology for professional reimbursement. They sponsored a project at Harvard University that was published in *JAMA* (*Journal of the American Medical Association*) in 1988 and resulted in Medicare shifting to resource-based relative value scale (RBRVS) payment methodology.[1] This was signed into law by President George H. W. Bush in 1989 and took effect in 1992. In anticipation of this implementation, the AMA established the Relative Value Scale Update Committee, better known as the RUC, in 1991. Ever since, the RUC has provided regular updates as recommendations to CMS, which are generally accepted and implemented. The RUC looks at new codes, and for existing codes, they look for changes in medical practice, coding, and the cost of the components that make up the RBRVS.

While health plan payments to providers have grown in complexity over time, the foundation of FFS payments remains fairly straightforward. The RBRVS sets the value of every CPT code relative to an index of 1, called a relative value unit (RVU). The RUC determines the relative value of specific codes by analyzing the physician's time, the overhead, and the liability associated with a particular procedure.

In general, CMS and commercial health plans embed the RUC-defined RVUs into their contracts and then offer a specific dollar amount per RVU as reimbursement. That dollar amount is called the conversion factor (CF). The simple result is that RVUs × CF = payment.

Unfortunately, many factors have come into play that substantially complicate the story. Since 1989, CMS has essentially adopted the RUC recommendations as the official source of their reimbursement for Medicare Part B. Health plans, though, are not required to follow the same methodology as CMS—even for their Medicare Advantage members. Because the RVUs get updated annually, there is generally some wiggle room for health plans as to the timing of those updates. Depending on the financial implications for a plan, there may be an incentive to drag their feet in implementing those updates. Beyond that, payers can modify RVUs from the RUC recommendations. As a result, there can be variation across payers and even within a single payer across lines of business in exactly how RVUs are employed. Since individual patient encounters often involve multiple procedure codes, the logic used to add modifiers and how those modifiers alter RVU calculations are subject to yet another layer of variation.

The growth in patient cost sharing has created an additional level of complexity. While co-payment rules are relatively straightforward, coinsurance and deductibles are not. The coinsurance can't be calculated until after the claim is adjudicated, so providers can't bill for it until after they receive the paid claim from the health plan. Deductibles are subject to timing issues. Since they depend on when a service was delivered, whether a patient has met their deductible is based on the timing of a particular service compared to other services. If a prior service has not yet been adjudicated, then it's possible that a patient's current encounter will not be subject to any deductible. Again, the provider is stuck waiting until claims have been adjudicated, and even then, there may be subsequent adjustments for delayed claims.

Providers with a clear understanding of the challenges and opportunities associated with FFS payments will be well positioned to make the most of current contracts. Perhaps more importantly they will have a strong foundation for negotiating optimal payment methodologies as they enter into value-based arrangements.

Key Takeaways

1. FFS payments are based on a contractually agreed-to conversion factor multiplied by the RVU of a given service.

2. Health plan flexibility combined with a wide range of patient cost sharing have driven significant complexity into this otherwise straightforward approach.

Recommendations

1. Make sure your billing department (or vendor) is keeping up with payment guidelines of each health plan.
2. Request periodic updates from health plans to anticipate changes in payment guidelines and create proactive billing strategies.

CHAPTER 8

What Happens to a Claim?

With an understanding of the basics of fee-for-service reimbursement, the issue at hand is to understand how a health plan actually pays a provider. This understanding should serve as the foundation for each provider's claim submission process and may also inform negotiations when payer contracts are up for renewal. While insurers traditionally include negotiated prices or fee schedules in their provider contracts, those prices are merely the starting point for managing actual payments to providers. In this chapter, we will follow a claim through a typical health plan's process to elucidate the variety of steps taken to avoid "overpayments" to providers.

In today's world of computerized submission of claims, many of the health plans' internal processes have been automated as well. The first software a claim will likely encounter is a filter that sits in front of the claims processing engine. These customizable filters can both drive efficiencies for the health plan and enable them to avoid regulatory time constraints on processing claims. This "preprocessing" software is used for an increasingly broad array of issues such as capture of quality metrics like body mass index (BMI), or to ensure that required clinical information is attached to a claim. From a regulatory perspective, a claim doesn't count as being submitted if it is rejected before it gets in the system. The clock doesn't start and it is not considered a "denial" if the claim is rejected at this point. This also saves money for the plan by avoiding the costs of processing claims that will need to be resubmitted.

A simple example might be that the filter would reject a claim for an annual wellness visit (G0438 or G0439) if the BMI is not included. The health plan needs that information to meet quality standards. By rejecting the claim before it even begins to process, the regulatory "clock" does not begin, and by sending it back to the provider with the specific information about why it was rejected, it removes the outreach burden from the health plan. Often this same filter can be used to identify and reject incorrect use of modifier codes as well.

The claims processing system is the primary engine that processes all claims for the health plan. This system pulls together all needed information about the member, the benefits, the specific service, and the specific provider contract and adjudicates the claim accordingly. This is where services that require prior authorization will be denied if there is no authorization in the system.

The output of claims processing is a preliminary reimbursement amount based on coverage, allowed amount, and co-pay, coinsurance, or deductible applied. For professional services, the allowed amount is the contractually negotiated conversion factor multiplied by the RVU value of the service(s) being billed.

The typical next step is for the claim to go through another set of software that is frequently updated based on ever-changing coding rules. This is generally referred to as clinical editing software. This software removes the need for frequent modification within the claims processing engine and instead takes the adjudicated claim and applies a regularly updated set of rules to ensure accuracy and appropriateness of the outcome. Something as simple as finding that there were three claims for knee replacement surgery on the same day might trigger this "highly unlikely" event to be denied, when the claims system itself did not pick up this discrepancy. This software enables modification of adjudication rules based on evolving CMS and industry practices for appropriate payment. Common examples include: two procedures on the same day on the same patient billed separately rather than with a modifier, inappropriate use of a modifier, billing outside the "normal" range for units of service, and so forth. This software will either reject the claim and force resubmission or reject part of the claim and provide partial payment. The clinical editing software is often vendor based, with the health plan paying licensing or subscription fees.

Because the typical health plan processes tens of thousands (if not hundreds of thousands) of claims per day, even a tiny percentage of modified claims can drive significant dollar savings for the plan. Because of this, it's not unusual for plans to employ multiple layers of clinical editing, often on a contingency basis with specialized vendors before final adjudication of each claim. In that case, after it goes through claims editing software the entire batch for the day may be forwarded to an outside vendor to go through their proprietary software. Often the vendor is paid a percentage of any incremental savings their software creates.

Even after the claim is paid, the health plans do not give up. They likely maintain an audit and recovery department that looks for unusual patterns of billing over time that are not picked up by clinical editing. They will typically use vendors, often several layered over one another, who request medical records and identify systematic or individual cases of inappropriate billing and recover money from providers.

A relatively new process in this arena is to use specialized vendors after clinical editing but before payment to avoid paying in the first place. An example would be an orthopedic vendor that has surgeons reviewing operating reports together with the claim to avoid paying for any billed service that is not documented in the surgical note. Since some facilities use standard charges for an operation without regard for what equipment was actually used, this approach has generated significant savings for payers.

Finally, health plans have a fraud and abuse unit that often gets referrals from audit and recovery but has their own software that identifies claims patterns that might represent fraud or abuse. In recent years, a collaborative process has been established across health plans and with government agencies where they share current investigations with each other. This has significantly increased the likelihood that providers with unusual billing practices will be identified and pursued.

For providers, it's important to maintain open communication with each health plan—to be aware of and prepared for any changes in claims submission rules. There may also be opportunities to negotiate the removal of "pain points" in this process when contracts come up for renewal. Given the level of complexity and pace of change in claims processing, as well as the number of plans in which they participate, it's not surprising that providers have increasingly turned to their own set of vendors to help with revenue cycle management in an attempt to keep up.

Key Takeaways

1. Health plans employ robust capabilities to efficiently process claims and avoid overpayments.
2. Health plans often include vendor services in their claims processing. Some vendors employ proprietary algorithms that the health plan is ignorant of. As a result, the plan may be unable to explain all payment denials to provider.

Recommendations

1. Request an in-service from major payers to explain their specific steps in claims processing.
2. Request clarity on clinical editing rules that are common to your practice.
3. Create process to incorporate health plan updates on claims processing changes and ensure a proactive adaptation of claims submissions.
4. Consider negotiating limitations on health plan claims adjudication into provider contracts.

CHAPTER 9

Payment Errors

When a health plan says a claim is lost or they send an incorrect payment, providers often feel like victims of an evil plot. In trying to decipher health plan motives it may be helpful to consider the scale and complexity of their operations.

Health plans must have claims processing systems that can accommodate more than 70,000 ICD-10 procedure codes and over 69,000 ICD-10 diagnosis codes.[1] Add to that the more than 10,000 CPT codes used for professional billing and the fact that those codes are not static. In 2022, there were 249 new codes added, 63 deleted, and 93 revised.[2] Those 405 changes all had to be incorporated into each health plan's claims processing system and cross-referenced with all of their contractually defined payment rules.

While it's true that automation goes a long way toward enabling management of this complexity, it's important to recognize some constraints on the payer side. Health plans invest enormous resources in their claims processing infrastructure, which means that replacing those systems with the latest technology is both expensive and extremely complex. Most of today's health plans exist as the result of multiple mergers and acquisitions. As a result, some still have different claims platforms in different geographies or for different lines of business. These legacy systems each have their own set of quirks that makes it virtually impossible to implement the exact same set of payment rules across all systems.

Another issue for health plans is the variation in their contracts with providers. As described in chapter 6, most health plans establish a single conversion factor for all providers in a geographic area and payments are calculated using standard RVU methodology. This is referred to as the "community fee schedule." When an individual provider group negotiates a deal that is not the community fee schedule, it drives significant complexity for payers. Every time there is a modification in coding rules, that change has to be applied and tested across all fee schedules to make sure it processes claims as intended. Just as with providers, compliance with regulatory changes sometimes requires manual work-arounds that add yet another layer of complexity to the process.

As mentioned in chapter 4, the past decade has also seen a dramatic rise in high-deductible health plans. Since the timing of claims submissions from various providers does not necessarily align with the timing of the services delivered, it's almost impossible to know in real time where a patient is relative to their annual deductible. While this is hugely problematic for providers (and patients) from both an administrative and cash flow perspective, even health plans with the best infrastructure to track claims and payments are faced with this same challenge around timing.

On top of all these layers of complexity, payers have the added challenge of volume. Consider a hypothetical health plan that has one million members. Based on Health Care Cost Institute reporting, the average American generates about 18 claims per year for health care services.[3] That translates to almost 50,000 claims per day for our hypothetical payer. Even if you assume a 99% accuracy rate for processing those claims, that means there are about 500 claims per day (182,500 per year) that have errors.

Clearly there is reason for providers to be frustrated and concerned about insurers' ability to make accurate, timely payments. That said, providers need not be concerned that they are being individually targeted by health plans. Given the volume and complexity of claims processing, from the payer's perspective picking on an individual provider would be the equivalent of finding the proverbial needle in a haystack. That said, providers can take action to improve the situation. For example, validating changes to fee schedules and maintaining open lines of communication with payers can help identify and correct errors before they become a problem. For those who haven't already done so, it's also worth considering use of a revenue cycle management (RCM) service. Vendors in this space diligently apply evolving regulatory guidance and individual payer contract terms to systematically ensure optimal, timely reimbursement for all services rendered. These vendors may also assess provider documentation to ensure providers are billing for the full value of services rendered and recommend specific contract terms that deserve consideration for renegotiation. At its core, a reliable RCM partner will manage the complexity, volume, and fluctuations in claims processing to minimize denials and ensure timely, accurate payments.

In the coming chapters, we will examine the functions and capabilities of a health plan, as well as their implications for providers.

Key Takeaways
1. Health plan payment errors are almost never intentional.
2. There are ways for providers to minimize the risk of being affected.

Recommendations
1. Validate all health plan fee schedule changes.
2. Maintain open lines of communication with health plans to understand their strategies, challenges, and actions in claims processing.
3. Consider use of an RCM vendor to keep up with the complexity, volume, and evolution of claims submissions.
4. When planning negotiations for payer contracts, identify pain points in the claims submission rules that might be modified.

CHAPTER 10

Health Plan Strategic Concerns

With an understanding of the functions and capabilities common across health plans, we can begin to identify strategic themes that drive their priorities. Particularly for providers entering into value-based contracts, understanding a health plan's strategic concerns can strengthen their ability to negotiate an optimal arrangement.

A high-level view of the country's five largest health plans reveals a theme that offers common ground that providers can employ as a foundation for collaboration. Each of these for-profit plans (United, Anthem, Centene, CVS/Aetna, and Cigna) has a mission statement whose central focus is to improve the health of those they serve.[1]

Where differences may arise with providers is in the how, not in the what. In general, insurers focus on improving access to health care services as their primary way of contributing to improved health. Furthermore, they focus on controlling costs and maintaining affordability as the primary mechanism for improving access. In a somewhat self-serving set of logic, they view growth in membership as evidence of success in achieving their mission. Historically, this approach has included three foundational strategic themes:

1. Keep total claims cost plus administrative costs less than total revenue (i.e., generate a positive margin).
2. Keep claims plus administrative costs lower than competitors'.
3. Maintain service levels to members and employers to avoid regulatory scrutiny and client dissatisfaction.

Strong execution of these three strategic themes has been fundamental for those health plans that have demonstrated long-term growth in membership. In this context, driving the efficiency of administrative functions is a high priority. There are two factors that underlie this strategic imperative. The first is the obvious one that impacts all businesses. Improved efficiency of core functions improves their competitive position.

The other, and perhaps less obvious, concern for payers is their medical loss ratio (MLR). Across the country this is variously referred to as the health benefit ratio (HBR), medical benefit ratio (MBR), and medical cost ratio (MCR). Regardless of the term used, the definition is the same (i.e., the percentage of health plan revenue that is expensed for medical costs). Therefore, health plan administrative costs and profit are not part of MLR. The ACA set minimum requirements for MLR for Medicare Advantage, Medicare Part D (Pharmacy), commercial small group products, and commercial large group products.[2] For each of these, plans are required to keep MLR at or above 85%, except for small group/individual products where the lower limit is set at 80%. In other words, at least 80 to 85 cents out of every premium dollar must be spent on medical services.

Driving administrative efficiency can both improve a plan's bottom line and simultaneously ensure the MLR does not fall below statutory requirements. The most common strategies payers employ to accomplish this include membership growth, automation, and process improvement. Partly because of the additional focus on MLR, plans may also be interested in transferring administrative functions to providers in order to pay through claims rather than administratively.

For health plans with a dominant local market share, certain other strategic concerns are predictable. These plans face the constant risk of another plan entering their geography. They understand that providers may be willing to accept lower reimbursement from a health plan with a tiny market share, as the marginal cost of accepting a few more patients is negligible. Lower prices combined with a tiny market share enable new entrants to offer lower premiums than the dominant player at minimal risk to themselves. The established plan will likely make significant concessions to a provider that is positioned to help a new entrant in return for their "loyalty." Loyalty is interpreted as tacit assurance that the provider will not agree to lower reimbursement from new entrants.

As noted in chapter 5, many health plans profit from selling "buy-up" programs to their large employer groups. They often sell their basic administrative services at or below cost, then make a profit with offerings such as wellness, enhanced utilization management, pharmacy management, and care management. Increasingly, management services organizations (MSOs) and other third-party vendors have been marketing these capabilities directly to employers, offering more attractive buy-ups than the health plans.

As providers develop capability and capacity in these functions, they are particularly well positioned to drive changes in their relationships with commercial payers. Providers can help payers lower both medical costs and administrative expenses. Transfer of payer's care management (see chapter 13) or utilization management (see chapter 11) dollars directly to providers shifts administrative expenses to a claims expense. This helps plans meet regulatory MLR requirements but might cut into the health plan's profits on their ASO buy-up programs.

If health plans view their UM and CM programs as a "product" they offer employers, then providers with mature population management capabilities can pursue the alternative strategy of offering those programs directly to large employers. With this approach, providers become a more direct threat to health plans. Initially, they can approach employers as a cost-effective alternative to health plan buy-up programs. If they can show employer groups how they can meet the needs of employees with improved outcomes and lower costs, the group may be open to a limited or tiered network that channels people toward a set of preferred providers. The logical extension of this strategy represents the biggest threat to health plans, the potential for a group of providers to exclude the health plan from large local employers by bringing in a silent partner and offering their own limited network insurance product. Chapter 22 is entirely devoted to a discussion of the risks and benefits of venturing into this "payvider" world.

As leaders understand the strategy and priorities of health plans in their geography, they can use their own evolving population health capabilities to ensure their contracts with plans reflect their full value. The threat of eventual disintermediation will likely drive traditional commercial insurers to engage in collaborative initiatives. In return for support of the payer's strategic priorities, clinicians can expect plans to provide the financial, operational, and data-analytic support needed to successfully transition to value-based care.

Key Takeaways
1. Almost all health plans include improving people's health in their mission statement.
2. Most health plans focus on controlling costs as a way to achieve this, since lower costs make access to services more affordable for more people.
3. Health plans prioritize reduction of their administrative costs.

Recommendations
1. Seek transfer of health plan functions to provider.
   a. Case management
   b. Utilization management
2. Request changes that reduce health plan administrative expenses:
   a. Exempting "low-utilizing" providers from prior authorization (gold carding) or targeting only "high-utilizing outliers" for prior authorization (red carding).
   b. Give Health Plan UM nurse direct access to EHR in return for elimination of requests for medical records.

CHAPTER 11

Analytics

The Affordable Care Act provided for the establishment of the Consumer Operated and Oriented Plan (CO-OP) program. These are nonprofit health plans that are governed by a member-dominated board of directors. By 2013, there were 23 CO-OPs offering coverage through the state or federal health exchanges. Even with substantial government subsidies, as of January 2021, only three remained.[1] This failure rate of 87% can be largely explained by the absence of a robust data set and analytic capabilities that left these start-ups at a disadvantage.

Not unlike most provider organizations, health plans consider their data one of their most important assets—the core of their value proposition. Health plans use their claims-based data set in at least four fundamentally different ways. In fact, they will often have separate analytic functions to meet their actuarial, financial, clinical, and quality-performance needs.

One of the major challenges that commercial payers face is predicting the future (underwriting). Plans that offer Medicare Advantage need to submit their benefit design and premium charges by June 1 for the following year. That means that with claims data from the first three to four months of the year, health plans are forced to predict what their costs are likely to be in the coming year. And the stakes are fairly high. If a plan overestimates future costs, they will likely charge a higher premium and offer weaker benefits than a competitor that accurately predicts the trend. The result will be a loss of membership to competitors. Typically, low-utilizing seniors are much more likely to shift to a lower premium product during open enrollment, leaving behind the sicker patients for the plan that has raised premiums the most. So not only can the plan lose membership, but it may also lose money on its remaining population due to this "negative selection." That dynamic can force plans into a downward spiral of continuing to need to raise premiums as the less sick among their members move to lower-cost competitors.

Alternatively, if a plan underestimates future costs, expands benefits, and minimizes premiums, they will likely experience unexpected growth in membership that may result in excessive losses for the year. While it is likely true that the new membership will be less ill than the average Medicare population, that is typically not enough to offset the losses related to underestimating costs. Let's look at an example to make the point. Suppose Health Plan A has 100,000 Medicare Advantage members with average cost and revenue of $600 per member per month (PMPM), or $720 million (M) annually. That plan predicts a 5% increase in costs for the coming year. They have a competitor that predicts a 3% increase. If the competitor is correct, that competitor could easily acquire 10,000 of Health Plan A's healthier members, adding as much as 2% to the cost trend for Plan A, thus "eating up" all of the profitability that might have been generated by overestimating expenses. Revenue will be $680M and so will costs (table 11.1). Even with an overestimate of cost increases, the entire profit is absorbed by the negative selection.

In the second example (table 11.2), the competitor correctly estimates the cost trend to be 7%. In this case, Health Plan A may gain 10,000 of that competitor's healthier members who actually are break-even with the 5% projection. The resulting revenue will be $831.6M versus costs of $846.2M, resulting in a loss of $14.6M. The important point here is that there are negative consequences to errors in either direction. The competitor in this example, by correctly estimating the cost trend, maintained much more stable financial performance with either a $1.2M gain or $1.4M loss.

While state requirements for submission of commercial insurance premiums generally come later in the year than for Medicare, this same challenge exists across all product lines except Medicaid, where benefits and revenue are both determined by the state. Parenthetically, this absence of flexibility on both premiums and benefits makes managing a Medicaid line of business extremely challenging for health plans. Their primary options are to focus on quality and regulatory compliance to maximize revenue and reduce payments to providers to control costs. But for all other lines of business, accurately predicting future costs is fundamental to success. As a result, health plans make significant investments in their actuarial team, which specializes in historical trends combined with relevant current experience and knowledge of potential market disruptions to calculate future costs. The larger the market share that a plan has, the easier it is for them to make accurate predictions. This issue is one of the main reasons it's challenging for start-up insurance companies to be successful. If there is a secret sauce in the health insurance world, it is actuarial proficiency.

Table 11.1. Potential impact of overestimating cost trend

	Year 1 membership	Year 1 costs	Predicted trend	Actual trend	Year 2 membership	Year 2 revenue	Adjusted trend	Year 2 costs	Profit/loss
Competitor	100,000	$720M	3%	3%	110,000	$815.76M	2.85%	$814.572M	$1.188M
Health Plan A	100,000	$720M	5%	3%	90,000	$680.4M	5%	$680.4M	$0

Table 11.2. Potential impact of underestimating cost trend

	Year 1 membership	Year 1 costs	Predicted trend	Actual trend	Year 2 membership	Year 2 revenue	Adjusted trend	Year 2 costs	Profit/loss
Competitor	100,000	$720M	7%	7%	90,000	$693.36M	7.22%	$694.786M	−$1.426M
Health Plan A	100,000	$720M	5%	7%	110,000	$831.6M	6.85%	$846.252M	−$14.652M

The absence of that proficiency is precisely the problem that CO-OPs encountered when they entered the exchange market in 2013. A good example is Health Republic Insurance of New York, established by the Freelancers Union.[2] Flush with subsidies from the government and mission driven to provide affordable coverage, but lacking claims data that might provide some historical compass for rate setting, they substantially underpriced the market in the very first year. Then, with only a few months of data from a fairly small population, they lacked the information that suggested changing course for the second year and so once again offered the lowest premium on the New York Exchange. As a result, by the end of that second year they had attracted a significant market share but found themselves in a financial hole from which they could not escape. By April 2016, they were liquidated by the state due to insolvency.

As critical as actuarial proficiency is to health plans, they can't operate effectively without real-time analytics focused on revenue and expense. Therefore, finance departments have their own analytic resource to close the books on monthly performance, understand year-to-date performance, and reestimate full-year expenses and revenue. To do this, health plans face a singularly difficult challenge. Most businesses have a very clear understanding of their expenses but have some uncertainty regarding revenue in the realm of accounts receivable, never knowing exactly how much they will ultimately have to write off. Health plans also have this issue, but they actually have a much bigger problem on the expense side related to the delay between when patients receive services and when the claims are submitted to the health plan. This category of expense is referred to as "incurred but not reported," or IBNR. The delay is so significant that for services delivered in January, it's not until sometime in April that enough claims have come in to have a clear picture of those expenses. As a result, IBNR is a plug number estimated by the finance analytic team to enable monthly closing of the books. Given the critical role of real-time financial analytics in managing any business, health plans function under the constant stress of being three months behind in understanding their performance. This leaves very little room for "midyear" adjustments to achieve performance targets.

Aside from the pure business side of the company, health plans' clinical teams need analytics of a different sort. Clinical teams use analytics to understand cost trends within each product line by service category, diagnosis, unit cost, and utilization. Clinical analytic teams also commonly examine both costs and trends compared to national and regional benchmarks. These analytics are focused on identifying actionable opportunities to reduce waste and ensure patient care is appropriate for their circumstances. They therefore seek specific services that are being used more frequently than the national average, and to understand which patients or providers are driving that variation. Alternatively, they will examine a subset of patients that are high-cost outliers and work to understand the clinical or demographic issues that are driving those costs. These same analytics are used to monitor the impact of health plan interventions intended to reduce or avoid costs. This type of analysis serves as the foundation for creating, modifying, and eliminating utilization management and care management programs.

The final major category of analytics for health plans is in the arena of quality metrics. This capability has been largely built over the past 15 years as Medicare and Medicaid have increasingly put health plan revenue at risk for quality performance. Typically, the revenue related to quality for these lines of business represents the difference between being in the red and being in the black. Today's health plans therefore have a dedicated quality analytics team. This team has the unenviable task of understanding the ever-changing and detailed specifications for every metric in the universe of Medicare and Medicaid quality measures (there are literally hundreds of them), anticipating changes in measures and benchmarks, and monitoring performance individually and in aggregate for each line of business. This team's work then serves as the foundation for building and managing programs to positively impact results.

While all four analytic functions within a health plan look to the claims database as the primary source of information (because they use that data in very different ways), there is often significant variation in reported numbers, depending on which team generates the report. Variation in specifications can make similar reports show very different results. It becomes a herculean task to crosswalk the different "sources of truth" and understand how each approach both produces value and is consistent with information derived from the other approaches.

As providers move down the path of value-based contracting, this entire analytic universe of the health plan takes on new and added significance. The health plan's struggles to crosswalk reports that originate in different areas may initially appear to providers as a lack of transparency, an attempt to confuse them, a sign of incompetence, or all three. While these four separate streams of analytics can be confusing, each plays a critical role in driving the success of a contract that puts providers at risk for quality and costs. The actuarial arm is critical to producing realistic targets for financial performance. If their cost or revenue projections are off, then the financial performance targets for the provider may not be realistic. The finance analytics provide information throughout a performance year to support providers in understanding the need for "midyear" adjustments to their work plan. The clinical analytics team has the most to offer providers in terms of specific insights into where and how to focus resources to reduce waste. Finally, the quality team can provide subject matter expertise to a provider's nascent population health efforts to ensure that quality data is captured and reported in a way that meets the requirements of the contract.

Key Takeaways

1. Health plans view claims data as a critical strategic asset.
2. Health plans tend to have multiple and siloed analytic functions.
3. There is often no "single source of truth" within health plan reporting.

Recommendations

1. Consider request for external actuary to validate health plan cost trends and targets.
2. Request dedicated resource from health plan finance to support operational understanding of monthly or quarterly reports.
3. Request health plan medical director and clinical analytics support to identify and track progress on areas of opportunity for cost savings.
4. Request in-service on health plan quality analytics as well as dedicated support for tracking at-risk quality measures.

CHAPTER 12

Cost Management Strategies

While commercial health plans have a complex role as the financial intermediary in health care, they are often perceived to have a singular focus on managing the cost of care. In this chapter, we will review the variety of methods they employ to do just that. A better understanding of each of these tactics will position providers to strategically respond to the challenges and opportunities inherent in managing cost trends.

At the center of a health plan's strategy to control costs are negotiated prices. Traditional fee-for-service contracts with providers are almost singularly focused on this issue. As a foundational business practice, health plans seek lower prices than their competitors on the assumption that they will be able to charge lower premiums for the same set of benefits if they are paying lower prices. In chapter 7, we examined in detail the tactics that plans embed in their approach to claims processing to protect the role of negotiated prices in controlling costs. In this chapter, we will focus on negotiated prices as an overall strategy to control costs.

While on the face of it negotiating discounts appears to be a straightforward and potentially effective tool, history has proven that it is anything but that. Professional fee schedules based on conversion factors and RVUs are somewhat predictable, but the problem with negotiated prices is that they fail to account for utilization or intensity of services.

The issue with utilization is straightforward. If a health plan negotiates a price of $100 for chest X-rays with a radiology group and the number of X-rays performed goes up by 10 percent, then the cost to the health plan will rise by 10 percent even with no price increase.

It's also important to understand the less obvious, but more profound, impact of intensity (we'll come back to utilization later in the chapter). A simple example can again be found in radiology. Say a radiology group is doing 5,000 chest X-rays annually, and 500 chest CTs at a negotiated price of $100 per X-ray and $500 per CT scan. The annual cost for chest imaging would be $750,000. Now in the following year, keep the prices the same and the total number of imaging studies at 5,500. A simple shift in services to 4,500 X-rays and 1,000 CT scans drives the total cost of imaging to $950,000—a 26.67 percent increase. As it turns out, this issue of substituting more expensive services for less expensive ones is a major driver of health care cost trends. In many instances, the added cost is clearly related to added value, but aside from the work of the Institute for Clinical and Economic Review (ICER), which focuses mainly on pharmaceuticals, little has been done to examine the added cost versus added benefit as intensity increases.[1]

With an understanding of intensity, it becomes clear that much of what is called "utilization management" by health plans is actually intensity management. Prior authorization for most services is less about reducing the number of services provided and more about driving that utilization to the lowest cost-effective service. In fact, these programs typically do both. In the aforementioned example, the goal of a health plan's radiology management program would be to both eliminate unnecessary CT scans (utilization) and avoid the shift from X-ray to CT scan where appropriate (intensity).

Most people think of prior authorization when they hear the term "utilization management," but health plans actually have three primary ways of attempting to mitigate the trends of ever-increasing utilization and intensity of services. It starts with benefit design, where co-pays, coinsurance, and deductibles are in place not only to offset costs for the payer but to give direct incentives to patients to avoid costly services. For example, significant cost sharing for emergency department encounters has been shown to drive people to urgent care or primary care as an alternative. Unfortunately, these cost-sharing schemes are very difficult to fine-tune, resulting in a variety of unintended consequences. We see this when people opt out of physical therapy programs that have a co-pay for every visit in favor of an expensive and sometimes risky procedure that has only a single co-pay. Similarly, co-pays for phototherapy services create a disincentive for patients with psoriasis to try this safer and cheaper alternative to injections of biologic drugs. Even more concerning is the contribution these benefit designs can have on health disparities. Studies have shown that cost sharing for ED visits is a safe and effective way to reduce unnecessary ED visits in our health literate population, but in lower socioeconomic groups this same benefit design can result in poor outcomes due to avoidance of truly necessary emergency department care.[2]

The primary mechanism health plans employ for managing utilization and intensity is prior authorization. This approach is typically reserved for expensive services that have high potential for overutilization. Health plans often look for variation in use rates of services among same-specialty providers in their network to identify areas of opportunity. For most of these services, the focus is on intensity as much as utilization, as often the service being reviewed is a new technology or a new use of an existing technology.

That said, prior authorization is actually used in a variety of ways and for a variety of purposes. Sometimes plans focus on high-volume rather than high-cost services. The goal here is simply to reduce or avoid unnecessary services. With physical therapy (PT), for example, plans often approve a certain number of services following an orthopedic procedure. If they can reduce the average number of postoperative PT visits by 10 percent, it generates significant savings for them. Some health plans will put in programs to create "speed bumps" for providers, with little intention of denying requests but refusing to pay if the process is not followed. This "gotcha" tactic is not common but has damaged the reputations of all health plans in the eyes of both providers and patients. Some states have made this illegal, requiring plans to pay claims if the service was medically necessary, even if the authorization process was not followed.

At the other end of the spectrum, prior authorization is used to ensure early identification of patients who might benefit from the payer's third approach to managing utilization—case management. In this situation, a payer may not even require clinical review and approval, but simply notification so they are aware of the patient's status. While there is minimal evidence that it works, the intent of case management as it relates to utilization is to support patients with complex clinical or social needs that might otherwise end up overutilizing resources. The idea is to support timely, appropriate care to reduce redundancy, ED visits, and other potentially avoidable complications.

More recent attempts to manage costs have been found in "centers of excellence" and "narrow network" strategies. There is actually good evidence that centers of excellence (with records of high volumes; dedicated, trained staff; and low complication rates) produce substantially better outcomes for many conditions, particularly surgical conditions, at significantly lower cost than any alternative place of service. An early example of this was found with the Whipple procedure for pancreatic cancer. The mortality rate for this procedure was four times higher in hospitals that only did one procedure annually compared to those that did ten or more.[3]

Narrow or tiered networks are another approach that some health plans have explored. By stratifying providers within each specialty by average cost per episode of care, health plans can select those providers with lower-cost profiles and create benefit designs that allow access to these providers with less cost sharing than the rest of the network. In many states, there are legal restrictions on health plans' ability to discriminate among providers in this way, but self-insured businesses are exempt from those restrictions.

The final mechanism for controlling utilization is alternative payment models with providers. The earliest attempt to do this might be the introduction of diagnosis-related groups (DRGs) for inpatient stays. Whether bundled payments, ambulatory payment classifications (APCs), or ACOs, the intent of these approaches is to align incentives between providers and payers to reduce unwarranted variation in care by sharing in the financial benefits and risks related to cost trends. While these approaches have yielded mixed results, there is clearly a commitment from federal and state governments, as well as most health plans, to continue down this path.

As providers focus on their health plan contracts, understanding each payer's approach to each method of managing costs becomes a critical context for negotiations. For plans that lean heavily on prior authorization, there may be opportunities for some or all of that accountability to be transferred to the provider. A simple example of this is "gold carding," where a provider is exempted from clinical review if they achieve an agreed-to rate of approval (e.g., –95 percent). This approach reduces administrative burden on both the provider and the plan. Another alternative to consider with a payer is a "red carding" program. In this approach, only providers who are high-utilization outliers for a particular service are subjected to prior authorization in the first place.

As providers move into value-based payment arrangements, opportunities in this realm can expand further. Early on, providers may actually benefit from expansion of health plan prior authorization programs, as they can drive cost savings that result in higher incentive payments. This can be particularly helpful if the plan controls costs that are not part of the provider's revenue. As a provider organization becomes more sophisticated in managing utilization and intensity, other opportunities arise. An example would be to eliminate prior authorization in return for embedded decision support tools in the EHR that facilitate the most cost-effective choices.

As providers begin to focus on managing cost trends, they will benefit from understanding their payers' strategies. The nuances of each payer's approach to cost management will uncover specific opportunities and challenges that merit attention in the negotiation process. Often a provider can complement or support health plan activities to improve their own performance in value-based contracts.

Key Takeaways

1. Intensity of service is a major driver of health care costs.
2. Health plans are ill equipped to manage high-volume, low-cost "waste" in the delivery system.

Recommendations

1. Channel patients to lower-cost providers.
2. Support increases in prior authorization for high-cost services/drugs.
3. Channel patients to lower-cost therapeutic equivalents.
4. Manage low-cost / high-volume services such as urinalysis or hematocrit.

CHAPTER 13

Quality

For health plans, there are two distinct quality issues with little overlap. The first one relates to the efficiency, validity, and reliability of their internal operations. Like any business, it is important for their daily functions to be accurate, reliable, and efficient. In health plans, this translates into a focus on continuous improvement of their large-scale functions. Customer service and claims processing are invariably the two biggest items, but other functions such as enrollment, sales, and contracting are fair game as well. In this chapter, we will explore the other side of quality for health plans: the quality of health care services that their members receive. In general, clinicians are trained to think of quality as good bedside manner combined with optimal patient outcomes. The payers' view of quality is much more concrete and has driven providers to follow suit.

Fifteen years ago, health plans talked a fair amount about the quality of care their members received, but they often had somewhat lackluster approaches to it. Some viewed it as a marketing issue, wanting to be able to advertise that they had the highest

NCQA ratings in their market. For many the focus was more on avoiding being noticed for poor quality by either low ratings or regulatory infractions. That is no longer true, thanks largely to Medicare and, increasingly, Medicaid. As these programs have tied significant components of health plan revenue to quality performance, and placed plans in competition with each other for those dollars, health plans have made significant investments to improve their ratings. To understand health plan quality strategies today, it's necessary to look at Medicare, Medicaid, and commercial lines of business separately.

For health plans that offer Medicare Advantage, Medicare star ratings have become a "make-or-break" issue. These ratings began in 2007 as a tool for consumers to compare health plans. Over the past decade, CMS has put a significant percentage of health plan revenue at risk based on their star ratings. Given the current financial impact of those ratings, most plans would be unable to sustain a Medicare Advantage presence with less than a 4-star rating. For a plan with 100,000 members, dropping from 4 to 3.5 stars would drive a revenue loss of greater than $30M or about 4%. On the other hand, the added revenue for going from 4 to 4.5 stars would only be about $2M. Four stars is really the sweet spot. In fact, some plans are afraid of achieving 5 stars. One of the "benefits" of achieving this maximum rating is that people can enroll all year round, not just during the two-month open enrollment period that occurs in the fall. Many plans believe this would result in sicker patients being more likely to enroll than those who are healthier, and this "negative" selection would end up hurting them financially.

When it comes to achieving a 4-star rating, a big challenge for health plans is that the ratings are competitive. As average performance on each measure improves, the target score for achieving each star rating rises as well. Benchmarks for most measures are constantly rising. Plans are therefore in a constant race to outperform their peers just to maintain their ratings. While the Medicare star program continues to evolve, the current ratings are based on three separate tools. There is a direct assessment of each health plan's quality performance, the Consumer Assessment of Healthcare Providers and Systems (CAHPS) scores, and the Health Outcomes Survey (HOS) scores.[1] Health plans have found that in order to succeed, they need to manage the entire universe of measures across all three of these categories.

The direct assessment is divided into two categories. The first category focuses on members' health care experience, using specific metrics related to screening and prevention services, care coordination, and frequency of follow-up for chronic conditions. The other direct measures examine overall satisfaction with the health plan, member complaints, call center service levels, and timeliness of appeals and enrollment.

The CAHPS survey can be a little confusing, as it has evolved into a large set of surveys that focus on different stakeholders such as hospitals, dialysis centers, nursing homes, medical groups, surgical centers, and so on. CAHPS actually began in 1995 as a program focused solely on assessing consumer satisfaction with health plans. The current program is run by the US Agency for Healthcare Research and Quality (AHRQ). There are four different health plan surveys: adult versions for both commercial and Medicaid populations and child versions for the same two categories. Each survey has about 40 questions that assess consumer satisfaction regarding services received in the prior 12 months.

The HOS is specific to Medicare and follows a random cohort of health plan members, assessing self-reported changes in their health status. Each year a random sample from each Medicare Advantage plan is selected, and that same cohort is then surveyed again two years later. Health plans are evaluated based on the change in outcome status reported from year one to year three. This survey is made up of about 70 questions that involve self-assessment of an individual's physical and mental health, health care, and living circumstances. Most of the questions request respondents to answer in the context of the previous four weeks.

Unlike Medicare, Medicaid quality assessment is managed at the state level. The result is enormous variation among the states in terms of what is measured, and what the rewards and penalties are for health plans based on those measures.

In states that have financial penalties or rewards based on quality, the health plan issues are similar to Medicare. Even in states that are already supporting value-based contracts for Medicaid providers, though, there tends to be less money at risk than in Medicare. Conversely, given the narrow or negative margins that most plans have in Medicaid, even small incentives matter. Unfortunately, while Medicaid may use measures that are similar to those used for Medicare and commercial lines of business, they are often not exactly the same. Because of the increased prevalence of certain diseases in the Medicaid populations, health plans tend to focus their quality programs on those diseases. Aside from prevalence, regulatory scrutiny typically drives health plans to pay particular attention to mental illness, substance use disorder (SUD), and HIV.

In some states, regulatory compliance measures are a significant component of Medicaid quality scores. Some of these measures put plans in the awkward position of being accountable for individual provider policies and procedures. One example from

New York State makes the point. If a provider is listed in the health plan directory as open to new patients, that practice must give an appointment to any new Medicaid patient with no questions asked. If the state makes a "secret shopper" call to a provider and the receptionist asks for prior records before making an appointment, the health plan is held accountable for having an "inaccurate" directory. New York State does not consider a provider's patient panel to be open to new members if prior records are required to make an appointment.

For the commercially insured, there are currently no health plan financial incentives related to quality. There are metrics and star ratings for exchange products but no dollars attached to those ratings. Quality ratings are not viewed as a powerful marketing tool unless the ratings are very bad. Some insurers do not even participate in NCQA accreditation for their commercial products. Others consider it part of their mission or a "table stakes" issue that requires investment.

As providers consider value-based contracts, particularly in managed Medicare or Medicaid programs, it will prove particularly useful to understand health plan performance and strategy regarding quality metrics. The payer will likely push providers to focus on those measures most likely to help them achieve or maintain optimal premiums from the government. Understanding the payer's challenges, opportunities, and priorities as they relate to these measures should inform the provider's strategy both in contract negotiations and operationally. Building effective collaboration on quality metrics can create a "win-win-win" scenario for patients, providers, and health plans. For a provider that is considering value-based arrangements in multiple lines of business, it is critical to understand the different metrics they are asked to be accountable for, as the number of measures can quickly become unmanageable.

Key Takeaways

1. For health plans, quality metrics are much more important in government programs than in commercial ones.
2. In order to maximize revenue from the government, health plans need robust quality programs that address the entire universe of metrics.

Recommendations

1. Link provider quality programs to health plan resources.
2. Support health plan quality and compliance priorities in government programs, even if they aren't performance measures in the contract.
3. Ask health plan to transition their quality resources to provider to convert administrative cost to claims cost and achieve better quality scores.

CHAPTER 14

Care Management

Even though health plan–based care management programs have been pervasive for many decades, it remains an ill-defined endeavor with little evidence to support its effectiveness. Because payers commit significant resources to it, understanding their specific approach in each line of business can help providers position their own care model to collaborate or compete with them.

Interestingly, most attempts to define care management come from outside the health insurance industry. One such definition was provided by the Health Industry Forum: "Care management programs apply systems, science, incentives, and information to improve medical practice and help patients manage medical conditions more effectively. The goal of care management is to improve patient health status and reduce the need for expensive medical services."[1]

Even though health plans are increasingly employing more digital capabilities in their care management programs, case managers have served as the foundation of this strategy from the earliest days of managed care. As far back as the 1980s, studies show that virtually all health plans employ case management as a technique to improve outcomes, reduce costs, and increase satisfaction of their members.[2] These resources have been focused on patients who are identified as high risk based on either utilization patterns, diagnoses, actual costs, or projected costs. That said, there is very little evidence to support the effectiveness of these interventions. Though somewhat dated, a meta-analysis published in the *Health Care Financing Review* revealed a history of mixed results and weak methodology in assessing care management return on investment (ROI). While there are studies to support the effectiveness of provider-based care management programs for certain chronic diseases such as heart failure, most published studies that demonstrate savings for health plan programs use pre- and post-intervention data to support cost savings. Regression to the mean, or the tendency for statistical outliers to drift back toward the average, is a major issue for high utilizers in health care. It renders "before-and-after" studies unreliable in assessing the financial performance of care management. In a more recent study published in *Health Services Research*, the authors conclude that "despite the belief in the success of PHM [population health management] programs, there is little evidence to suggest that they significantly reduce health care costs."[3]

Ironically, despite the lack of evidence to support health plan case management as a cost-savings technique, it has persisted as a mainstay of capabilities for virtually every payer. Given this weak scientific foundation, it's not surprising to see significant variation across health plans regarding the structure, function, and goals of their care management programs. Most of this observed variation is driven by the differences that exist in the benefit design, funding mechanism, demographics, and clinical prevalence across payers and across products. The simplest and most profound distinctions are seen among Medicare, Medicaid, and commercial lines of business. While further variation is driven by health plan philosophy and the specifics of benefit designs, an understanding of each of these categories will suffice to give providers a sense of how they might collaborate, complement, or compete with health plan care management programs going forward.

Medicaid members, almost by definition, have significant challenges in the realm of social determinants of health (SDOH). While Medicaid shares in the high prevalence of diseases such as diabetes, COPD, heart disease, and hypertension, it also carries a disproportionate share of chronic illnesses such as sickle cell anemia, HIV/AIDS, SUD, and mental illness. Health literacy challenges also tend to be prevalent in this population. As a result of these factors, Medicaid lends itself particularly well to care coordination support, so most health plans that administer Medicaid benefits have a robust care management capability. In general, these programs consist of a staff of registered nurses (RNs) often augmented by social workers, nutritionists, and pharmacists. More recently, many plans have added community health workers, trusted members of the community they serve, who are able to locate certain individuals and facilitate their connection to a case manager. Typically, behavioral health care management is carved out and performed almost exclusively by social workers. The goals of case management in Medicaid are straightforward. The case manager works with the member to facilitate connection to a PCP (or the appropriate specialist) and ensure obstacles to care are addressed and care gaps are closed. In addition to process measures, health plans will measure ED visit rates and potentially avoidable hospitalizations as outcomes of these interventions. In some states, the department of health for the state requires that plans demonstrate connections to, and support for, individuals who are considered particularly vulnerable, such as those with HIV/AIDS. In those cases, health plans must demonstrate both qualitative and quantitative evidence of these programs to avoid penalties.

In Medicare, case management programs can serve two somewhat separate purposes. Often a plan will leverage these resources to support gap closure to maximize star ratings. An example might be a robocall campaign targeting women who are due for bone densitometry. To strengthen this type of outreach, the recipient of these calls can opt for a warm transfer to a nurse case manager who can help assess the need and connect the recipient to a provider. Because there is so much money riding on Medicare star ratings, these low-intensity uses for case managers are deemed worthwhile. At the same time, the frail elderly are a major driver of utilization and cost in Medicare. They often have complex needs, with multiple chronic illnesses, polypharmacy, and significant SDOH challenges. In these situations, a case manager can provide ongoing support and coordination of care in order to avoid ED visits, inpatient stays, and bad outcomes. Of course, even with these patients with complex needs, case managers will work to close gaps in care related to star measures. Success in Medicare for health plan care management is measured by reduced ED visit rates and acute hospitalizations, as well as improved medication adherence and star ratings. Because of the frequency of receiving thank-you notes from Medicare members for case management services, health plans also see case management as a marketing and member retention tool.

Case management in commercial products tends to attract a much lower level of investment from health plans. This population tends to be the healthiest and the least in need of support regarding SDOH. Additionally, to date there are no financial incentives or penalties for quality performance in commercial products, so in most cases service-focused utilization management programs tend to receive a disproportionate share of health plan resources. Despite this context, health plans do invest in care management for commercial populations to meet the expectations of employers. Benefits managers, brokers, and consultants all want to see that the plan is identifying and supporting high-risk members to drive early intervention, optimize outcomes, and avoid costly complications. For large, self-insured employer groups, consultants will often recommend a carve-out of care management to niche vendors, especially if the plan cannot demonstrate comparable customized programs with demonstrated savings. This dynamic places health plans in a difficult position. Arguing that the evidence is weak for the benefit of case management when the consultant is taking the opposite stance can create or exacerbate a credibility issue between the plan and the employer group. Establishing a robust case management program, however, will only increase costs for both the plan and the employer. Unfortunately, plans often end up focusing on demonstrating "engagement rates" and using the same sloppy analytics as the care management vendors to show the savings that accrue from their care management program. These are typically before-and-after numbers that are quite impressive but for a regression to the mean—a concept unfamiliar to many HR benefits managers, who may not have a strong background in statistics.

It's worth noting the differences among Medicare, Medicaid, and commercial lines of business in terms of investment. Generally, plans will target 2% of their covered population for case management services. As commercial members are less complex than Medicare and Medicaid, one full-time equivalent (FTE) can manage about 600 cases annually, leading to a staffing ratio of one FTE per 30,000 members. In contrast, the complexity of the government program subscribers drives a ratio of one FTE per 10,000 members for Medicare and Medicaid.

Even though health plan case managers will often reach out to provider offices to help arrange appointments or transfer pertinent clinical information, most providers have little awareness as to which of their patients are even receiving case management services from their health plan. As providers enter into value-based contracts with payers, the details of the payer's care management program take on new significance. Based on the numbers stated earlier in the chapter, a provider group with 10,000 patients in a Medicare or Medicaid contract, or 30,000 patients in a commercial contract might request dedicated health plan care management support as part of their agreement. If the provider can quantify the engagements and impact of their own care management functions, they might be able to get the health plan to eliminate their own care management and transfer those dollars to the provider. This is particularly true for government programs where care management does not affect health plan revenue. Providers can also reasonably argue that there is better evidence for the value of care management resources embedded in the delivery system than in a health plan.[4] Ultimately, transfer of care management resources into the delivery system will enhance the provider's ability to effectively manage their most complex patients, positioning themselves for success in value-based arrangements.

At a minimum, as providers develop their own care management capabilities there is value in transparency between the payer and provider. If both parties understand the target populations, interventions, and measured outcomes of each other's programs, they can work to avoid redundancy and drive synergies over time. This transparency should also translate into real-time sharing of data regarding the who, what, and why of those being managed.

Understanding the approach that health plans are taking with their care management resources may help providers build a more effective capability themselves, get material support from health plans, and improve KPIs for both quality and cost management. If a provider is so inclined, it can even help position them to market these capabilities directly to large, local employer groups.

Key Takeaways

1. Health plans invest in care management despite the paucity of evidence for its effectiveness.
2. Health plans invest more in care management for government programs than commercial ones.

Recommendations

1. Compare health plan care management goals to provider's.
2. Work with health plan to build transparency between health plan and provider care management programs.
   a. Coordinate programs to avoid redundancy or conflict.
3. Request dedicated health plan case managers for attributed population.
4. Request transfer of health plan care management resources to provider.

CHAPTER 15

Health Plan Committees

In 2015, New York State enacted the Nurse Practitioners Modernization Act, which removed the requirement for a nurse practitioner (NP) to have a collaborating physician agreement once they had 3,600 hours of practice experience.[1]

Primary care physicians spend three years in residency before being eligible for board certification, and this New York State law allowed NPs to be fully independent with less than two years of posteducational clinical experience. With this change in the law, health plan credentials committees were pressed to reevaluate their training and certification requirements. Not surprisingly, community physicians who sat on those committees generally opposed this "lower" standard for NPs. Because of their participation, physicians were able to vote to have the health plan maintain higher standards than the state required. Whether or not one agrees with the decision, it is a good example of the influence that providers can generate through participation on health plan committees.

Health plans generally employ a variety of standing committees in addition to their overall contracting strategy to build, support, and manage their network of providers. Health plans that seek NCQA accreditation—and most do—are required to demonstrate provider involvement in governance and operations. As a result, many of their standing committees include providers from the network. Understanding the role of each committee can position providers to take advantage of opportunities to influence health plans on matters that might affect their practice. This type of committee participation fosters connections that can prove particularly useful in the context of value-based contracts.

Each health plan has its own approach to governance and network management, but there is generally some overlap between the two. Often there is both physician and hospital representation on boards of directors. Many health plan boards have a subcommittee focused on quality that typically consists of a preponderance of providers. This represents a great entrée for a provider to get involved in health plan governance. Sometimes plans will also create provider advisory boards designed for a range of purposes. They might be used to create and govern a specific new program, or they might serve as a sounding board to get input and feedback on current or planned provider facing initiatives.

For all managed care products (HMO, PPO, EPO), health plans are required to credential providers, and most, if not all, have credentialing committees that are made up of providers in the network. Participation gives providers not only influence over who is in the network but, more importantly, input on credentialing policies. The NP policy cited at the beginning of this chapter is an important case in point.

For large provider groups that have NCQA certification, it's worth considering delegation of credentialing. In this case, a provider organization can credential all of its own providers and just submit the credentialing documentation to health plans. Most health plans are happy to delegate credentialing wherever NCQA permits.

Another important health plan committee is medical policy. This committee is made up of network providers across a broad array of specialties. The purpose of the committee is to determine when and if new technologies, or new uses of existing technologies, have enough evidence to be covered as standard, nonexperimental services. Participation on this committee gives providers significant influence over if, when, and how a new technology will be covered by the health plan. For example, as new technologies such as robotic surgery and neutron beam radiation therapy are introduced, this committee reviews the literature, seeks input from appropriate specialists, and determines whether the evidence suggests it is a safe and effective alternative to the current standard of care. The plan generally has a small staff of clinical researchers that compiles all peer-reviewed literature and provides a report with "staff" recommendations to the committee, but ultimately the committee decides. NCQA requires that all medical policies be reviewed and updated at least once annually, creating an ongoing opportunity for members to react to evolving evidence as well as obtain input from the provider community. Votes taken in a medical policy committee translate directly into criteria for prior authorization programs, and ultimately into the claims processing for if, when, and how a service/technology will be reimbursed under member and provider contracts.

Somewhat analogous to the medical policy committee is the pharmacy and therapeutics (P&T) committee, which focuses on drugs covered under a member's prescription benefit. This committee generally reviews all classes of drugs annually and determines tier level, prior authorization, and step therapy rules for each class of drugs. Specialists and pharmacists on the committee have significant influence over both strategy and policy within each drug classification. While most medical policy committees are focused almost exclusively on clinical evidence regarding safety and efficacy, P&T routinely considers cost in their deliberations as well. Since providers may have a direct or indirect financial interest in various medical technology innovations, health plans have struggled with the concept of directly assessing the relative value of new technologies in this forum. Prescription drugs, though, have almost no direct financial impact on providers. It is also apparent that there is greater clinical redundancy across medications than for other medical technology. It is much easier to compare two different ACE inhibitors than to compare an MRI to a CT scan. As a result of these differences, cost is a routine part of the deliberation regarding drugs and in fact is a primary driver to tier placement, step therapy, and prior authorization.

Individual plans may have other standing committees or provider-facing programs that represent opportunities to create more meaningful connections, drive alignment toward value-based care, and ultimately exercise greater control and influence over the future of medical practice. Providers can advance both their organization's and their personal position in the communities they serve through effective engagement with their preferred health plan.

Key Takeaways

1. Health plans have a variety of committees that include provider representation.
2. Many of these committees have substantial influence over policies and procedures that impact providers.

Recommendations

1. Consider participation on medical policy committee if your practice regularly adopts new technologies.
2. Consider participation on credentials committee if your practice is growing and adding a variety of specialties or levels of training.
3. Consider participation in quality or other board committees if there is a dominant health plan in your geography.
4. Keep abreast of ad hoc health plan committees that may align with practice strategy and goals.

PART III

Contracting

CHAPTER 16

Health Plan Contracting 101

Historically, provider contracting has been a foundational capability of health plans. In contrast, until the rise of HMOs toward the end of the twentieth century, most provider organizations were small practices that generally were in a "take it or leave it" situation when it came to contracting. As a result, health plans have capacity, capability, and resources in the contracting space that put provider organizations at a disadvantage. On top of that, because health plans are purchasing services from providers, antitrust laws generally apply to providers, not plans. The recognition of clinically integrated networks (CINs) in addition to independent physician associations (IPAs) as legitimate negotiating entities has created a more level playing field on which to negotiate with health plans. While most providers will see value in bringing external expertise to support their negotiations, a foundational understanding of contract attributes and variables will serve them well.

For small practices in urban settings, professional services contracts with health plans leave little room for negotiation. If a particular practice does not create a geographic or service gap in a payer's network, then providers have very little leverage in contracting. From the payers' perspective, reliable execution of individually customized contracts with small practices is problematic, as they typically have tens of thousands of providers in their network. Consistency in their contracts serves as the foundation of reliable, timely, and accurate payment of claims. As noted in chapter 8, variability in provider contracts is an important driver of claims processing errors.

As a provider organization becomes large enough to create a gap in a health plan's network, it is immediately positioned to negotiate a more customized contract. In rural areas, these may be fairly small practices. For primary care or multispecialty groups, a good rule of thumb is 10,000 patients. With 10,000 patients covered by the same health plan, a practice is large enough to enter into a value-based contract and might be able to negotiate a customized fee for service contract as well. That said, even small practices with no obvious negotiating leverage can sometimes find opportunities to participate in payer-initiated pilot programs, or even to approach a payer with an innovative idea for a pilot program.

Before a provider begins contract discussions with a health plan, it is critical for them to have a clear understanding of their own strategic position and goals. The provider organization's strengths, weaknesses, opportunities, and threats set the foundation for any contracting strategy.

Once a provider has a clear view of how value-based care fits into their mission, vision, values, and strategy, assessing potential health plan partners is essential. For primary care or multispecialty groups, panel size with a given payer should be the first filter for stratifying health plans. As mentioned previously, a panel of 10,000 patients is somewhat of a magic number. This number of patients with a given health plan is enough to ensure credible risk on various performance measures. It provides for large enough denominators to ensure valid, nonrandom quality metrics. Although it would require significant reinsurance to cover random high-cost events (stop-loss), it's also large enough to support reasonable cost estimates based on past history or risk adjustment.

It is a fortunate few providers that already have trusting relationships with a health plan. In the absence of that, it's critical to assess the desire and capacity of each plan to function as a partner. Much can be learned from requesting a meeting with local or regional health plan leaders. Without C-suite-level conversations, though, it's virtually impossible to evaluate the strategic intent of a health plan and to identify common interests and goals that might serve as the foundation for a successful value-based arrangement. One way to think about this is to place a double meaning on the word "value" in value-based contracts (VBCs). In order to be successful, the provider and payer must share "values" that align their efforts to increase "value" for their customers/patients.

These leader-to-leader meetings should focus on high-level strategic goals so that both sides can determine where there are common interests that can be foundational to any contract. For providers on the path to value-based care, this is the first step in identifying health plans that have the potential to become trusted partners in that journey. Just as important is identifying those plans that don't share this common vision.

Contracting elements will vary somewhat depending on the specialties involved, and value-based contracts are inherently more complex than traditional fee-for-service (FFS). Every element of a contract is important, including clarity about what is omitted.

Often template contracts from health plans begin with a definition of terms. Language in those definitions is typically phrased to protect the health plan, sometimes to the detriment of the provider. Terms as simple as health plan "revenue" and "expense" likely require clarification. They can be influenced by a wide variety of factors such as prior-year adjustments, regulatory penalties, subrogation, and delays in annually expected increases in premiums and fees. These details can have material impact on the provider and should be clarified in the contract. Careful reading and questioning of definitions can go a long way toward avoiding future misunderstandings.

The duration of the contract is particularly important. The journey into value-based care requires commitment over time combined with a willingness on both sides to learn and adapt. The term of the contract itself and the timing of updates to performance measures in the contract should meet the operational capabilities and strategic goals of both parties. Since predictability is important to health plans, providers should be able to expect substantial concessions in return for long-term loyalty.

It's difficult to overstate the importance of a governance clause in value-based contracts. Typical traditional FFS contracts don't have specific governance clauses and may contain language like "sole discretion" regarding certain specifics. Sole discretion language reflects the intent of the plan to have unilateral control, with no consideration of joint governance to clarify ambiguities or resolve issues that aren't explicitly covered. The closest these contracts come to a governance clause is to have language regarding dispute resolution, often focused on a process for arbitration, with clarification of how the parties bear financial responsibility for its cost.

The overall intent of value-based contracts is to transform the business model of health care from a focus on maximizing revenue to maximizing value. For that transformation to be successful, health plans need to change as much as provider organizations. A governance clause that ensures joint oversight for managing the contract provides a fundamental underpinning of success. Ideally, this clause should create confidence that there will be regular meetings between leaders of both parties during which challenges and opportunities within each organization and between the two are explored and resolved. These meetings should be structured to support ongoing alignment and mutual support to drive success. In a successful value-based contract, everyone wins—the health plan, the provider, and, most importantly, the patient.

In another departure from traditional FFS contracts, VBCs will have a clause dedicated to quality performance. The first element of quality to consider is how it relates to finances. Options range from simply meeting a quality threshold to qualify for financial incentives to a direct, formulaic impact on upside and downside financial risk. The former is usually framed as a gateway where gainshare is either achieved or not based on meeting the quality target. The latter implies that gains or losses are modified by quality performance, in that better performance drives a bigger upside and smaller downside, and vice versa. This clause must also clarify the specifics of how quality performance is scored. Pass/fail versus partial credit needs to be determined both for individual measures and for the impact of overall score on the financial terms of the contract.

Ultimately, either the contract or an appendix should include the template for quality measures: how many measures, how they are weighted, how targets are established, and whether and how partial credit is achieved. Targets can be an absolute number, a benchmarked percentile, an improvement from baseline, or some combination of these. Typically, how overall quality performance ties to financials is in the financial clause of the contract, but no matter where it's located it needs to tie back logically to all of the elements of the quality clause.

Many of the details of the quality clause may be provided as an appendix to the contract, making it easier to update on a periodic (usually annual) basis. These details will likely include the specific measurements, weightings, and targets for the coming year. The quality clause should include an illustrative example that delineates the calculation of scoring, showing a hypothetical baseline, target performance, actual performance, and cumulative score.

A critical component unique to value-based contracts is the set of specifications that determine which patients belong to a particular provider (i.e., the attribution logic). For CMS-sponsored ACOs, there are a couple options available to providers, but they are clearly defined by CMS.

As providers move into similar arrangements with commercial health plans, they are faced with a much broader range of attribution logic. Because of this variability, it's critically important to understand the specifics of each health plan's proposed approach. Generally, for HMO products the assigned PCP determines the attribution, but for PPO and other insurance products, there is no assignment. Some formulation of claims-based use of primary care services is employed. It is in the details of this formula that health plans will likely demonstrate variability. Aside from the attribution logic itself, an agreement on timing of attribution should be codified as well. When the cohort is determined, if and when attribution is updated, and whether the same rules are used for both quality and cost attribution are all material issues that should align with the capabilities of both parties. See chapter 17 for a more in-depth review of attribution issues.

Finally, we come to the financial terms of the contract. In many ways, all the other elements of a value-based contract set the stage for the financial agreement. The financial terms of a contract are by far the most variable and complex component across value-based arrangements. The specifics of what is included depend heavily on which line of business is involved. For managed Medicare and Medicaid arrangements, the financial terms are typically based on a percentage of premium target. In the case of commercial agreements, it's more common for historical and projected cost trends to be employed to set expense targets. This one difference drives the need for a significant level of customization, even between two agreements with the same payer. For example, while percentage of premium arrangements demand rigorous attention to the details that define both revenue and expense, budget-based commercial agreements are singularly focused on expenses, but with added levels of complexity not generally seen in government programs.

The provider's level of maturation within value-based arrangements should be determinative of whether and how much upside and downside risk is included.

The mechanism and timing of incentive payments should also be clearly delineated. See chapter 17 for a deeper discussion of this issue.

Once the detailed specifications of calculating financial performance are worked out, the contract should include a sample calculation that demonstrates how each variable, including the quality performance, contributes to final results.

Overall, the complexity of how financial targets are set, what is included and excluded, and how risk for the provider is mitigated necessitate expertise at the negotiating table that can ensure the terms are realistic and aligned with the group's short- and long-term strategy. For most providers, it makes sense to invest in outside support for this expertise.

Another important consideration in value-based contracting is to take a phased approach. It can be very helpful to both parties to implement an agreement in the first year with little or no financial risk. This allows both parties to establish a baseline and observe actual performance as a foundation for setting meaningful and achievable targets going forward. It is a good test of both health plan and provider readiness, but, more importantly, an opportunity to build trust before introducing substantive financial risk. Providers will learn about the health plan's willingness and capability of sharing data, and the extent to which the health plan provides dedicated support resources. Both sides have an opportunity to demonstrate good faith in matters such as verifying attribution, researching questions, and resolving differences.

If the plan is committed to a provider's long-term success, they will not only agree to this phased approach but may be willing to build enhanced payment into this phase for new capabilities such as a population health platform. This would most likely be a sort of loan where future savings would pay back the health plan before savings would be shared with the provider.

If the early phase is managed well, both parties can enter into a true risk arrangement with confidence that governance, attribution logic, quality measures, and financial terms are structured to drive continuous improvement and sustainable success. In the coming chapters, we will explore in greater depth a more nuanced understanding of various components of value-based contracting.

Key Takeaways

1. Health plans have robust contracting expertise.
2. Traditional contracts typically protect health plans at the expense of providers.
3. Value-based contracts are much more complicated than traditional FFS contracts.

Recommendations

1. Strongly consider using a consultant to help with a value-based contracting strategy and tactics.
2. Keep notes on all conversations with the health plan as they can play a key role in resolving future disagreements.
3. Make joint governance and dispute resolution top priorities.
4. Seek multiyear phased approaches to increases in gainsharing and downside risk.
5. Ask for illustrative examples to clarify defined terms.

CHAPTER 17

Value-Based Budgeting

For Medicare ACOs, there's little room for negotiation. Even large provider organizations are forced to accept terms offered by the government. Value-based arrangements with commercial insurers present an entirely different opportunity. Though there is very little wiggle room for health plans in certain elements of the contract, there are many issues available for providers to negotiate to maximize the likelihood of success and sustainability.

For providers entering into commercial contracts that include upside and downside risk, there will likely be a contractually agreed-to total cost target that serves as the defining mechanism for financial performance. For managed Medicare and Medicaid arrangements, the target will likely be a percentage of the premium, while in commercial contracts it will more likely be a budgeted expense target. While this discussion focuses on the commercial track, the concepts apply to percent-of-premium arrangements as well. The contract should outline all factors that contribute to defining that budget target, both qualitatively and quantitatively.

The foundation of the budget lies in the clear delineation of the population for which the provider will be accountable. The early value-based arrangements that started in Massachusetts focused only on HMO populations. Since everyone with HMO coverage has an identified PCP, attribution was straightforward. With the inclusion of other coverage categories such as PPO, attribution became a challenge that drew comparable but varying solutions across payers. In general, it's in the provider's interest to include all patients that have an active chart with them throughout the performance year. Unfortunately, health plans, whatever formula they use, are pretty much locked into it, as any variation in logic across agreements would likely result in the same person being attributed to more than one PCP at the same time. This redundancy is unacceptable to health plans, as they would be doubly at risk for those individuals.

For their members who don't have an assigned PCP, plans generally have a formula that includes a "look-back" period for each of their subscribers, counts primary care encounters, and weights them based on both encounter type and recency to establish a PCP attribution for each individual. Understanding the details of a health plan's attribution logic is a critical first step in the budget process. A longer look-back period with less weighting of more recent visits creates a "stickiness" for patients with their PCP. In this situation, a patient who transfers into a practice after regularly visiting their prior PCP may not attribute to that new practice in the first year. This also implies that a patient who leaves a practice early in the year may continue to attribute to that PCP throughout the year even though they no longer go there for care.

A shorter look-back period with heavier weighting of recent visits can correct for these challenges but also results in a higher turnover rate with a risk of patients disappearing and reappearing in attribution updates.

An often-overlooked issue related to attribution is that typically 15%–20% of health plan members are unattributed, that is, they have no identified primary care provider. While some of these people have no PCP because they are under the ongoing care of a specialist for a chronic disease, the overwhelming majority are healthier people who just haven't gone to a PCP within the "look-back" period. The other group that tends to be unattributed are healthy women of childbearing age who use their OB-GYN as their primary care provider. Health plans benefit greatly from these unattributed members as they tend to be profitable, and none of those profits get shared with providers under value-based contracts.

Multispecialty provider groups provide a great example for managing this issue. First, they can identify patients in the care of their specialists who don't have a PCP and get them connected to a PCP in their group. Second, if they have their own OB-GYN department, there are two possibilities. One is to follow the same approach as other specialists and refer unattached patients to a PCP. The other is to negotiate with the health plan to add attribution logic that includes OB-GYNs as long as a patient is not attributed to a PCP.

Timing of attribution is another important component and may be more open to negotiation than the attribution logic itself. There are a variety of options regarding when attribution is finalized. Understanding the extremes of attributing either at the beginning or end of a performance year will reveal the underlying implications of various approaches.

Finalizing attribution on the first day of a performance year carries significant advantages for providers to consider. The year begins with clear understanding of exactly which patients within a practice are in the denominator for measurement of both quality and financial performance. This is a straightforward approach that is easy for frontline physicians and staff to understand, and it feels fair to have the entire year to impact everyone in this population.

There are some challenges associated with finalization of attribution on the first day. Patients who newly attribute to a practice after January 1 will not be part of the attribution, even though they have been active patients with the practice for the entire year. Remember that even with a short look-back period, a newly attributed member will have already had encounters before that attribution occurs. The larger issue for many practices is for those members who change providers during the year. Unless there are specifics in the contract that enable removal of patients from the attributed cohort, practices remain accountable for patients that are no longer coming to see them. A corollary issue for health plans is when an attributed patient loses or changes coverage to another payer during the course of the year. If there is significant turnover in coverage, then the cohort could shrink considerably during the year.

If this approach is used, it's important to have clear language in the contract regarding why, how, and when patients are removed from attribution with consideration of a process to reassess if turnover rises above a certain level. For providers with relatively small populations, this erosion of their accountable cohort can reduce reliability of quality indicators and increase financial risk. While those issues are less serious for larger groups, they might still experience a reduction in their overall risk/reward from a shrunken cohort.

In contrast, imagine an arrangement where the attribution is finalized at the end of the year. This solves the problem of reducing cohorts due to turnover either at the practice level or at the level of the health plan. It also incents providers to reach out to their attributed patients and keep them connected to the practice so they don't become unattributed before the end of the year. Unfortunately, this approach results in a lack of clarity as to just who is included in both budget and quality performance metrics throughout the course of a year. Essentially all performance metrics are estimates, with uncertainty about both numerators and denominators until year's end. This ambiguity creates both practical operational challenges and significant communication challenges for provider leadership to their frontline staff. These challenges can undermine credibility between the provider and the health plan. Unless otherwise specified in the contract, this methodology removes patients who die during the year from the attributed population, thus removing the incentive for providers to focus on end-of-life care. Closing gaps in care for those people who attribute late in the year may be a problem as well. No matter what timing is decided on, it's important for both parties to work through hypothetical examples, clarify the unintended consequences of their approach, and include measures to mitigate those issues. As this can be a significant source of friction between the provider and payer, a clear process for oversight of this issue, including dispute resolution, should be considered.

Comparable to the detailed specifications of attribution, determining what constitutes an expense and when and how those numbers are finalized is critical to a successful budgeting arrangement. As these issues are worked out, a general principle to keep in mind is that the more expenses are excluded or limited in the budget, the lower both the risk and the opportunity for the provider will be. For providers considering global budgets, it is important to take the time to consider the services to be included. A practice needs to apply its knowledge of its own capabilities to ensure it has some influence over costs that are included in the budget. For a provider that has no OB-GYN group within their practice, for instance, excluding pregnancy and delivery costs from the budget should be a serious consideration.

The timing and allocation of expenses are also important. If a service is subject to subrogation (an alternative source of payment), there should be clarity about how that is or is not included. In the absence of clearly delineated accounting, the health plan might count these as expenses and "ignore" the fact that they are getting reimbursed by the third party, arguing that it's revenue rather than expense mitigation. Likewise, prior year adjustments and penalties for late payments should be accounted for within the contract.

Another important component of expenses is prescription drug costs. For both managed Medicare and commercial arrangements, a significant portion of an attributed population will have prescription coverage through a different payer than the health plan providing medical coverage. If prescription drugs are included in the budget, then it's useful to understand the size of the population for which these expenses will be excluded. This may also be important for quality measures that involve medication compliance, as it is likely those data will be lacking on attributed members with alternative drug coverage.

With clarity about the population and the delineation of expenses, a budget is generally established by the health plan's actuarial department (see chapter 10). The plan should be able to share the data and explain the approach that led to their projection of costs for the coming year. It's also important to consider if there is a known disruptive technology that requires special consideration. This occurred when sofosbuvir (Sovaldi) was introduced at the end of 2013 and added billions of dollars in costs for 2014, that had not been accounted for in actuarial calculations.

Given that budgets for value-based contracts tend to be set for a calendar year, another consideration regarding the annual budget target is seasonality. Dividing an annual budget equally over 12 months is problematic. Winter months are higher cost, but if a large portion of the population has high-deductible coverage, actual claims costs will be depressed early in the year. How out-of-pocket expenses are accounted for therefore needs to be considered. High-deductible plans also result in a fourth-quarter spike in elective procedures as more subscribers reach their deductibles and rush to get elective procedures before their benefits reset in the new year. A provider could get a false sense of security based on performance in the first half of the year, and then end up with a "surprise" in the fourth quarter that substantially undermines their financial performance. To mitigate this concern, health plans can provide seasonally adjusted estimates month by month of expected versus actual incurred expenses and should have monthly updated year-end projections that transparently incorporate assumptions related to seasonality.

A correlate of seasonality is the variable annual impact of influenza. As budgets are often set based on a projected overall cost trend, this one issue can have a material impact. If an early influenza season that peaks in December is followed by a late influenza season that peaks in February, then that year-over-year trend will be higher than expected. Conversely, if that pattern is flipped, the trend will be suppressed. If the relative severity of

Table 17.1. Financial impact of timing and severity of influenza,
per member per month

	Year 1	Year 2	Delta
First quarter	$0.25	$2.25	$2.00
Fourth quarter	$0.75	$2.25	$1.50
Total	$1.00	$4.50	$3.50

those two flu seasons aligns with these timing issues, the impact on trend will be further amplified.

Estimates of the direct impact of seasonal flu on health care costs in the United States vary from one to three dollars PMPM.[1] Let's assume $2 PMPM as the average; $1 PMPM for a mild season, and $3 PMPM for a severe one. Calendar year 1 includes an early mild flu season impacting its first quarter and a late severe flu season impacting its fourth quarter. The second year has an early severe flu season. The overall impact is a delta of $3.50 PMPM (table 17.1). For an attributed population of 10,000 people, that's a $540,000 impact on expenses—just from influenza. This is an issue that deserves annual attention in setting budget targets and may also warrant definition of a process to adjust a budget if the fluctuation exceeds a predetermined amount.

The combination of attribution, definition of expenses, pharmacy issues, and seasonality makes construction of value-based budgets particularly challenging. Since provider organizations tend to have no actuarial capacity and the health plan produces all the data that's used, providers should consider employing an actuarial consultant to independently review the budget.

Key Takeaways

1. Patient attribution serves as the foundation of value-based budgets.

2. "Expenses" is a complex term that requires clear delineation.
3. Factors such as seasonality can materially impact cost trends.

Recommendations

1. Consider an actuarial consultant to independently review budgets annually.
2. Make sure that the risk and reward in the budget is aligned with operational competencies.
3. Ensure that the budget is straightforward enough to explain to frontline physicians and staff.
   a. Ask health plan for help with communication of budget.

CHAPTER 18

Incentive Payments

As providers consider participation in value-based contracts with commercial insurers, it is important to understand each health plan's capabilities and preferences for incentive payments, that is, any payments to the provider that are in addition to their earned fee-for-service payments. There is a natural tendency to focus on incentive amounts, but it is equally important to consider how and when the incentives will be paid.

As explained in chapter 6, traditional payments for professional services are based on a negotiated conversion factor multiplied by the RVU rating of each service. Occasionally, health plans will modify RUC-generated RVUs in response to local needs. An example might be a shortage of rheumatologists resulting in an increased RVU for joint injections (CPT20610). This type of modification is the exception that proves the rule, as health plans generally follow nationally established RVUs, taking their lead from Medicare.

The simplest way for payers to make incentive payments is to increase the conversion factor. This may make sense for relatively small incentives early in the value-based care journey but requires careful tracking and management to support more sophisticated arrangements. With inherent uncertainty in estimating the number of services to be rendered, it's challenging to achieve a precise incentive amount. An additional issue is that these incentive dollars are folded into standard reimbursement in a way that disconnects them from the activities and accomplishments that produced them. This methodology is often used in early phases of VBCs, where there is "pay for process" rather than "pay for outcomes." A health plan may agree to increase the conversion factor incrementally in return for the provider submitting quality data, achieving NCQA certification, or taking some other steps toward value-based care. This approach can help those providers gain the experience and infrastructure needed to transition into more mature value-based arrangements.

Sometimes a health plan will find an unused or minimally used code related to care management and create a specific reimbursement for that code. In this circumstance, there would be an auditable contractual agreement about how the code will be used by the provider to assure payments are aligned with the intent of the incentive. This method is seldom used as it creates complexity for payers that is quite challenging to manage. Similar to CF adjustments, the exact dollars are somewhat unpredictable.

For set-amount payments, health plans employ a variety of options. The most obvious approach is for the plan to make direct payments to a provider for the correct amount when that payment is due per the contract. As a most effective way of reinforcing behavior, some plans have used this approach and actually hand-delivered quarterly incentive checks and thanked the providers in person. While apparently straightforward, this creates a challenge for health plans, particularly in their commercial line of business. Self-insured employers will generally refuse to pay for health plan costs that are not directly attributed to a claim for one of their members. If audited, health plans therefore could be faced with eating these costs as purely administrative expenses.

To get around this, payers have found creative ways to tie payments to claims. One is to use the aforementioned bump in fee schedule and discontinue the bump when the owed amount is reached. A variation on that approach is to employ the bump in fee schedule and reconcile at the end of the year for the next year's fee schedule adjustment. If a hospital system is connected to the provider, the health plan can add a self-imposed tax on all inpatient stays for the remainder of the year, based on the expected number of hospital admissions. This also requires a reconciliation process and will artificially increase the apparent inpatient expenses for those months that the incentive payment is included. This increase in cost can have a confusing and even material impact on cost trends. The contract should therefore include a specific description of whether and how incentive dollars will be handled in performance calculations and budget setting.

Partial capitation is another potential solution. Here the health plan makes monthly payments for each attributed member, and the amount of those payments is calculated based on the total incentive amount. Since these tend to be small amounts for each patient, the challenge is to create a claim for them. The provider and health plan need to be able to maintain an up-to-date list of attributed members and the health plan needs to be able to generate claims for that roster of patients (roster payments) rather than individual claims for each patient.

The challenge of roster payments notwithstanding, partial capitation offers significant advantages for providers. As the

COVID-19 pandemic revealed the inherent risk of a complete dependence on FFS revenue, partial capitation provides a manageable transition strategy for diversifying revenue. Imagine a primary care group with 10,000 patients that average 2.5 visits per year. At $80 per visit, the practice generates $2M in annual revenue. A break-even conversion might involve a monthly prepayment of $5 per patient combined with a 30% reduction in reimbursement for visits. In this scenario, the provider would receive $50,000 monthly as a prepayment, with FFS making up the other $1.4M over the course of the year. This blended payment method would stabilize the provider's revenue stream by dampening the impact of variability in patient encounters.

Over time, a higher percentage of the payment could be converted to these monthly fees, and those payments could be risk-adjusted as well. Any services deemed to be "more is better," such as screening and prevention, might remain fully FFS, while acute care, monitoring of chronic conditions, and follow-up care could be fully "capitated." By gradually diminishing the focus on encounter-based services, practices would have time to adapt workflows to include virtual visits and population management while reassessing their long-term space requirements and staffing models. This gradual approach also enables both payers and providers to learn as they go, so they can pause, accelerate, or reverse course as needed.

This payment model enables a gradual shift to a value-based business model, affording providers time to manage the financial transition in parallel with the evolution of their clinical and operational strategies. Another advantage is that it remains independent of a provider taking risk on cost and quality performance metrics. At any point in this conversion to a hybrid prepayment model, performance payments can easily be integrated as a simple adjustment to the monthly per patient fee. Ultimately, this approach rewards providers for maximizing the efficiency and effectiveness of their services to patients. They can set themselves up for success by maximizing gainshare opportunities related to cost control, clinical quality, and patient satisfaction, even as they create opportunities to efficiently grow their patient base.

The primary challenge with this approach is reconciling the payments to individual benefit designs. How these payments connect to co-pays and deductibles would have to be clearly delineated and likely would require modifications to those benefit designs to accommodate capitation.

The most extreme departure from fee-for-service is to move to global capitation. Under global capitation, the provider is paid a predetermined, often risk-adjusted amount for each attributed patient and is at financial risk for all services received by those patients—hence the term "global." Risk can still be mitigated under global capitation by simply placing limits on potential losses and gains for the provider. This is often referred to as a "risk corridor." With the failure of so many IPAs in the 1990s that were under capitated HMO contracts, this approach fell from favor. As today's large provider organizations develop the information and operational infrastructure to effectively manage the cost and quality of care, build the assets to tolerate risk, and find payers that are able and willing to collaborate in driving performance, global capitation may once again become an attractive alternative for everyone involved.

Key Takeaways

1. Health plans vary in their capabilities and preferences when it comes to the mechanism of incentive payments.

2. Transitional payment models that blend FFS with incentive payments can send mixed messages to frontline providers.

Recommendations

1. Seek understanding of each health plan's payment capabilities and preferences.
2. Seek more frequent incentive payments that are visibly tied to operational successes.
3. Moving to some form of partial capitation, even in a cost-neutral way, can lower financial risk by diversifying revenue.

CHAPTER 19

Risk Mitigation

As providers evolve their own capabilities and confidence in managing the financial risk inherent in value-based contracts, adjusting contract terms to align with their risk tolerance will require ongoing attention. The intent of value-based contracts is for providers to share in the financial risk for a population, but only for the risks over which they have some influence or control. There should be provisions in the contract to protect the provider from random risk, sometimes referred to as insurance risk.

The most direct way to mitigate this risk for providers is to include stop-loss (also referred to as reinsurance) in the contract. Stop-loss insurance is designed to limit the provider's financial risk for unexpected, extremely high-cost claims. In determining the appropriate level of stop-loss, there are two major elements to consider. First is to determine where to draw the line. In general, the larger the population at risk, the higher the dollar amount for stop-loss should be placed. It may also be useful to go back to the provider's strategic plan and values. If, for example, focusing on end-of-life issues is a priority, it may be unwise

to set a low bar for stop-loss. It is estimated that for the Medicare population, about 25% of Medicare annual spending occurs
in the last six months of life.[1]

A focus on improving end-of-life care might generate significant cost reduction for a set of very high-cost claimants. If
stop-loss is set to take effect at $100,000 and a program focused
on end-of-life care reduces the average cost from $200,000 to
$150,000, then the provider would not get credit for those
savings.

In addition to determining the dollar amount at which stop-
loss occurs, the details of how it is applied require delineation.
Are all costs eliminated from both budget and expense? Are only
costs over the stop-loss eliminated? If the latter, are those costs
totally eliminated, or does the provider remain at risk for some
small percentage, typically 10%, of additional costs? As these details can have a material impact on the provider's upside and
downside potential, they deserve careful consideration.

Depending on how stop-loss is structured in the contract,
there may actually be a charge to the provider for this "reinsurance." In that case, the provider may want to shop around to
ensure the amount being charged is reasonable.

Another mechanism for adjusting the level of risk in a contract
lies in the details of how the financial risk corridor is structured,
that is, the magnitude of total upside and downside risk for the
provider. In general, providers should expect to have symmetri-
cal risk so that in order to lower downside risk, there would be
a concomitant decrease in upside potential.

The issue of whether and how to include risk adjustment into
a value-based contract is as important as it is complex. In government programs where financial targets are a percentage of
premium, there is inherent risk adjustment in that individual

premiums are driven by the disease burden of each patient. The two key challenges inherent in reliance on this approach are data capture and time delay. Health plan premiums for Medicare Advantage are based on the prior year's risk score for each enrollee. If a patient with long-standing diabetes does not have an encounter coded with that diagnosis during the year, then diabetes will be removed from the calculation of their risk score. From a timing perspective, if a patient has a new diagnosis in January, it will not be reflected until the following year, even though costs for that diagnosis will be incurred throughout that current year.

In both Medicare Advantage and managed Medicaid (a commercial insurer functions as MCO for Medicaid), the provider role in risk adjustment becomes a critical component of value-based contracts. Because the financial targets for these arrangements are typically a percentage of premium, maximizing revenue to the MCO (premium) benefits the provider just as much as managing medical expenses. Since risk adjustment for each member is based on diagnostic codes submitted to the payer *each calendar year*, the providers can ensure optimal premiums to the health plan by pursuing annual visits for all patients with chronic diagnoses and submitting claims with proper coding of all diagnoses.

For commercial arrangements that involve a budgeted expense target, there is also some level of risk adjustment built into the standard actuarial approach to estimating future expenses. The natural progression of disease burden for a given population over time is embedded in the actuarial calculations that create these targets. Essentially, there is an assumption that added disease burden and increases in cost due to new technology will continue at a similar pace going forward as they have in recent years. In this context, it is important to consider whether there is a disruptive technology that requires special consideration. As mentioned in chapter 16, this occurred when sofosbuvir (Sovaldi) was introduced at the end of 2013 and added billions of dollars in costs for 2014 that had not been accounted for in actuarial calculations.

Some plans might be willing to add a further adjustment into the budget where they apply a risk adjustment algorithm to the population over the course of the year and the budget isn't finalized until the final adjustment is made at the end of the performance year. These adjustments are typically based on diagnostic coding similar to that described previously for government programs. While providers may be attracted to this methodology as a way to make sure they get "full credit" for the disease burden of their population, this approach creates its own challenges. Imagine a multispecialty group practice in an urban setting. It is likely to have a higher-than-average disease burden. If that practice is expanding into surrounding suburban areas, it would benefit from an "unadjusted" budget as it experiences an influx of healthier patients. The other problem with this attempt to improve accuracy is that the provider doesn't know what their target budget is until the end of the performance year. It's difficult to plan, motivate, and execute actions around a nebulous target goal.

As mentioned in chapter 15, it's critically important to have a well-designed governance process embedded in any value-based arrangement. Providers should look to the governance process together with dispute resolution to help monitor and manage performance. These elements create a path forward to resolve issues where unintended risk is being placed on the provider. A further safeguard would be to include a "force majeure" clause in the contract—a "contractual provision which excuses one or both parties' performance obligations when circumstances arise which are beyond the parties' control and make performance of the contract impractical or impossible."[2] While potentially helpful, these clauses are no guarantee of protection from unforeseen circumstances, as the precise language is unique to each contract and there are varying degrees of enforceability across states.[3]

Ultimately, aligning the level of risk in a contract with the providers' capabilities and goals is a complex task. Given the rapid and sometimes unpredictable changes in the health care landscape, it requires expertise combined with a dynamic and diligent approach over time.

Key Takeaways

1. Risk mitigation is a dynamic, ongoing task in the context of value-based contracts.
2. There is a wide range of options for risk mitigation.

Recommendations

1. Seek health plan partners that are willing to calibrate provider risk to align with the group's capabilities and goals.
2. Maintain focus on risk mitigation both operationally and contractually.

PART IV

Opportunities and Obstacles in Value-Based Care

CHAPTER 20

Price Transparency

In the absence of price transparency, providers that are at risk for cost of care are at a huge disadvantage. In today's ACO and ACO-like agreements, providers are incentivized to drive waste from the system but are unable to guide their patients to the most cost-effective alternative without knowledge of cost or effectiveness. The cost of everything from an MRI to an outpatient surgical procedure can vary dramatically among providers, even within a relatively small geographic region. This is particularly true across hospital systems, where charges for various services have evolved over decades. As more and more individuals have coverage that includes deductibles and coinsurance, consumer demand for transparency is growing, and yet the tools made available for them by health plans are woefully inadequate.

This particular health care conundrum can be understood through the lens of "reimbursement." Providers and health plans both refer to payments to providers as reimbursement, not prices. Historically, and generally to this day, providers render services to their patients, then afterward submit a claim to the health plan for reimbursement for their costs. Often the provider doesn't even know exactly what they will get from the health plan until after the claim is adjudicated. This isn't surprising given the often unpredictable combination of services provided within a single encounter and the vagaries of health plan rules regarding the use of modifiers in claims submissions. Additionally, we now have a catalog of more than 70,000 procedure codes and 69,000 diagnostic codes that each can be tied to and impact payments. Benefit structures include deductibles and coinsurance so that the exact total cost of a service and the timing of that service in relation to any other services rendered are integral to determining the actual payment. A simple system of "reimbursing" a percentage of charges for services rendered has evolved, over a century, into a labyrinth that few can understand, let alone navigate.

In addition to this complexity, there exists a market dynamic that further undermines attempts to create price transparency. Many provider contracts have a clause that prevents either party from divulging anything about the financial terms between the two parties. The desire to keep this information secret generally comes from both the health plans and the providers. Health plans fear that if the financial terms of their provider agreements are known, then all providers will seek to match those that are paid the most. Providers fear the opposite—that they will be forced to accept lower payments in order to match their competition.

Contrary to this desire of both health plans and providers to maintain secrecy about their contracted rates, as consumers have borne an increasing financial burden through coinsurance and deductibles, they have demanded some level of price transparency. Most health plans now make a "cost estimator" tool available to their members so they can get an idea of the price of a service from different providers. These tools come with a disclaimer and are typically framed as a price range, not a specific price. Providers, even in value-based contracts, are typically contractually prohibited from using these tools to guide referral decisions unless initiated by a patient.

The government has begun to step into this space with a final rule published in late 2020 requiring health plans to implement increasing levels of price transparency over the next three years.[1]

An initial list of 500 common services will need to be available through an online, self-service tool showing members their cost share liability in real time. More importantly for providers, plans will be required to produce regular reports showing negotiated rates and historical payments for all medical and prescription benefits. When this requirement is fully implemented (scheduled for January 1, 2024), it will dramatically improve a provider's ability to help their patients make cost-effective decisions about their care, saving patients out-of-pocket costs while at the same time building greater opportunity for gainsharing in their value-based contracts. For providers that tend to be cost drivers, such as teaching and research institutions, this transparency represents a challenge as well as an opportunity. Those providers will be well served to negotiate payments that simultaneously account for their unique value and enable them to maintain competitive prices for routine services in their primary service area.

Key Takeaways

1. Both health plans and providers are resistant to price transparency.

2. Providers are in a unique position to guide patients to lower-cost, high-quality service options.
3. Government intervention offers hope of change.

Recommendations

1. Independent ambulatory care providers should push health plans to provide price transparency.
2. In light of transparency, teaching and research institutions should reassess their pricing structure.
3. In the absence of complete transparency, ask health plans for relative costs of certain services, even if it's just a one-to-four-dollar-sign indicator.

CHAPTER 21

Subrogation

Whereas the lack of price transparency is clearly an obstacle to success in value-based contracts, subrogation can cut both ways. Ignored or handled poorly, it can both complicate and compromise a provider's financial performance. If appropriately accounted for contractually and well managed operationally, subrogation can represent a significant business opportunity for many practices.

According to *Merriam-Webster*, subrogation is "the assumption by a third party (such as a second creditor or an insurance company) of another's legal right to collect a debt or damages."[1] In health care, it generally pertains to any situation where a patient's primary insurer is able to transfer responsibility for payment to another party. It is estimated that about $15 per person per year is potentially subject to subrogation. For a health plan with a million members, that's $15M. For a provider group with 10,000 patients, that is $150,000 annually.

To understand the implications of subrogation for providers, it's important to look at a variety of scenarios. Orthopedic surgeons are often the most familiar with subrogation, stemming from injuries that occur in car accidents or are work related. For car accidents, the automotive liability insurance typically is responsible for payment. From the payer's point of view, the subrogation opportunity is important because they wouldn't have to pay the claim, and from the provider's perspective payment from car insurance often means they are able to get paid at charges rather than at their discounted, contracted rates with health plans. The issue is very similar with work-related injuries, with workers' compensation coverage replacing the role of automotive liability insurance.[2]

Another situation where subrogation comes into play is when coverage changes during an episode of care. Say, for example, that a patient is hospitalized on December 26 under Insurer A and has already met their deductible. When the coverage shifts to Insurer B on January 1, assume the patient is still in the hospital and the new coverage has a $500 deductible. Since the patient was admitted while under coverage from Insurer A, in most states that insurer is liable for the entire hospitalization and may even be liable for costs attributable to that admission diagnosis for up to a year.

In general, subrogation is a payer-to-payer issue where the primary insurer (Insurer B) provides immediate coverage for whatever services a patient receives and then seeks reimbursement directly from the other source of payment (Insurer A). Nevertheless, both patients and providers can still get caught in the middle. Even if Insurer B pays the claim, they will not pay the $500 deductible. Both the patient and the provider can be left hanging with regards to if, how, and when Insurer A pays that $500.

To make matters worse, the laws regarding subrogation are variable from state to state. Some states specifically prohibit various forms of subrogation, such as health care costs that are otherwise covered benefits but are the result of a motor vehicle accident or court order.[3] If that isn't confusing enough, employer groups that are self-insured for their employees' coverage are exempt from these state laws and allowed to pursue subrogation.

On the positive side, subrogation also applies in the context of expenses related to recalls of medical devices. In this case, the manufacturer is liable for all costs related to complications from or replacement of the recalled device. As health plans are often unaware of which members are affected by these recalls, the provider can play a significant role in identification and referral for subrogation, and health plans should be willing to provide incentives to that end.

In value-based arrangements, subrogation takes on even greater significance, because both the provider and payer can benefit from ensuring that all potentially subrogated payments are realized. This will reduce overall costs for the contracted health plan and therefore increase gainsharing opportunities. In effect, the provider can receive subrogated revenue without it counting against their cost target. Of course, providers need to make sure that their contract with the payer requires that subrogation-related revenue be used to offset expenses in assessing the provider's performance. Health plans should be willing to include this in their contract language as they directly benefit when providers offer early identification of patients who may have subrogation issues.

Key Takeaways

1. Subrogation can represent both an opportunity and a threat in value-based contracts.
2. Subrogation opportunities vary significantly by specialty.

Recommendations

1. Ask the health plan to delineate and estimate the total value of subrogation opportunity of your attributed population.
2. Ensure contract language accounts for the expense reduction for the health plan that results from subrogation.

CHAPTER 22

Pharmacy Benefit Management

Just as subrogation can represent both a barrier to success and a significant opportunity, so too can the inclusion of the pharmacy benefit in value-based arrangements. Even as pharmacy costs represent a relatively painless opportunity to generate savings that contribute to gainsharing opportunities, variability, complexity, and accelerated adoption of expensive drugs can create significant challenges for providers.

While plans use vendors to support and enhance their capabilities, they all tend to have core functions that include customer service, network contracting, enrollment, sales, and claims processing. When it comes to pharmacy benefits, the picture becomes murky. Some plans own and manage their pharmacy benefits in a manner analogous to their medical benefit products; some contract for most, if not all, of their pharmacy benefit management; and some have settled on hybrid approaches. That means that some plans have their own pharmacy benefit management (PBM) capability, some contract out to an external PBM, and some only contract out to get the network and price discounts but have their own contracts with pharma and do their own utilization management. This variation is invisible to patients and providers at first blush but accounts for part of the mind-numbing complexity of often-contradictory rules across a patient population.

Unfortunately, this layer of variation across payers is perhaps the least confusing aspect of prescription benefit issues for providers and patients. The difference in how Medicare, Medicaid, and commercial insurance products are regulated means that even within the same health plan the formularies, tiering, step therapy, and prior authorization rules will be significantly different for each line of business. On top of that, it's not uncommon for self-insured employer groups (greater than 60% of the commercial market) to carve out pharmacy benefits to a completely different PBM than their health plan offers, driving yet another layer of variation among commercially insured members with the same health plan.

Because patients carry health insurance cards that are branded by who is providing their medical coverage, it's not obvious to providers or consumers that pharmacy benefits are often managed under a completely independent set of benefits and by a separate entity from the health plan, the PBM. Due to consolidations and mergers, 75% of today's PBM market share is held by three companies: Optum Rx, owned by United Healthcare; Caremark, owned by CVS/Aetna; and Express Scripts, owned by Cigna.[1] These three companies not only manage pharmacy benefits for their parent organization but also contract with other health plans to provide some or all of their pharmacy management needs. The result for providers is that two patients with the "same" health insurance can have completely different pharmacy benefits in terms of product tiers, in-network pharmacies, and authorization rules.

There are three major tactics that PBMs employ to manage pharmacy benefits. At the foundation of any PBM is their contracted network of pharmacies, through which they seek discounts on their charges for the prescriptions they dispense. Traditionally, a health plan might "shop" for the PBM with the largest discounts in their catchment area.

The second key strategy for a PBM lies in their direct contracts with pharmaceutical companies. Here they negotiate for discounted prices or rebates as a way of reducing potential costs. Oftentimes, these contracts are tied to the third approach taken by PBMs: the tier placement and use management rules they put in place. A typical contract might give a PBM a meaningful discount on a particular drug in return for making it the only drug among its competitors in the lowest tier or requiring a trial of their drug first (step therapy) before allowing a competitor brand (as well as some other prior authorization requirements). These contracting schemes are a major driver of confusion and frustration for providers and patients alike. The same drug can be in different tiers with different health plans and can even flip positions with competitor drugs over time as PBMs update their contracts.

The past decade has seen the rise of yet another player in the pharmacy space—the specialty pharmacy. Originally a designation mainly for those drugs that required special storage or preparation capabilities that were not present in all retail pharmacies, it has evolved into a focus on particularly expensive drugs, no matter the storage or preparation issues. In today's market, PBMs contract with a narrow network of specialty pharmacies in order to concentrate their volume in pursuit of deeper discounts on these most expensive drugs. Because these medicines are typically thousands of dollars per month, even a marginal discount can make a big difference.

Prescription drug costs and use patterns can have a major impact on providers in the context of value-based contracts. Understanding the details of a health plan partner's pharmacy benefit management strategy is critical to effective management of the consequent risks and opportunities.

As an example, consider a value-based contract with a health plan that has 10,000 commercial attributed members. Based on national averages, it's likely that 6,000 of those members are under an administrative services only (ASO) model. If half of those who are self-insured choose a different PBM to manage their pharmacy benefit, then only 7,000 of the attributed members have pharmacy benefits through the contracted health plan. If the contract includes pharmacy costs for all 10,000 members in the budget, it creates significant complexity for providers. The health plan should be able to provide good estimates of cost trends, helpful support for savings opportunities, and timely reports on utilization and cost for the 7,000 members they manage directly. For the other 3,000 members, providers are likely to experience variability in estimations of cost, availability of data, timeliness of reports, and, most importantly, variability in formulary design and content.

While drug costs can represent "low-hanging fruit" to reduce cost trends in VBCs, this complexity in benefit design and management can completely undermine a provider's ability to set reasonable budget targets and execute operationally on plans to use "preferred" drugs. Significant sophistication is therefore required to navigate both the contractual and operational issues that result from inclusion of pharmacy benefits in commercial value-based contracts.

Key Takeaways

1. Health plan pharmacy strategies often diverge from their medical benefits.
2. This divergence drives enormous complexity for providers.
3. Pharmacy represents a unique set of risks and opportunities for providers in value-based contracts.

Recommendations

1. Clarify each health plan's pharmacy benefit management operational structure.
2. Request report that delineates attributed members who have a pharmacy carve-out.
3. Clarify frequency and timeliness of pharmacy reporting for both carved-in and carved-out membership.
4. Separate pharmacy trends from medical trends in the budgeting process.

CHAPTER 23

On Becoming a Payvider

As providers consider their journey toward value-based care, it's worth understanding potential end states that might serve as a guidepost. For some groups, such as single specialty, maximizing the potential of an effective bundled payment strategy might serve as that endpoint. For primary care groups, it could be a partial or global capitation model. For large multispecialty groups, clinically integrated networks, or large hospital systems, becoming a payvider becomes a realistic possibility.

In the preceding chapters, we examined the complexities of a successfully functioning health plan. For providers considering a payvider strategy, there is clearly a level of capability, size, experience, and expertise required that demands time, effort, and resources to achieve. The varying regulatory environments across Medicare, Medicaid, and commercial insurance products by themselves are almost impenetrable to the uninitiated. The data and analytic capabilities for underwriting, operations, cost management, and quality metrics require both special skills and an adequate repository of claims data to make accurate projections. Building and interfacing with a provider network from contracting and provider relations to claims processing and cost management requires experience, knowledge, capacity, and relationships that are again foreign to most provider organizations. With an appreciation of just how big of a hill this is to climb, we can now examine what it means to become a payvider—with all the attendant opportunities and risks.

In its simplest form, a payvider can be understood as a single organization that functions as both a health plan and a provider. Viewed from a traditional health plan perspective, the health plan actually owns the providers in its network. Conversely, from the providers' perspective the provider organization builds or buys a health plan capability in which they serve as the exclusive or primary network for that plan's policyholders.

In practice, payviders are often not structured as a single organization. Kaiser Permanente (KP) stands as perhaps the most enduring example of a payvider in the United States, serving more than 12 million members across 8 states plus the District of Columbia.[1] The Kaiser model consists of three separate companies: Kaiser Foundation Health Plan (KFHP), Kaiser Foundation Hospitals (KFH), and Permanente medical groups (PMG). The contracts among them include mutual exclusivity clauses that effectively render them a payvider. All medical services for KFHP are provided by the PMGs, and PMGs only provide care to KFHP members. Additionally, in those geographies where Kaiser owns the hospitals, those hospitals only serve KFHP members and are staffed by Permanente physicians. This level of interdependency forces an alignment among these three stakeholders that is virtually unattainable in a traditional setting. Each stakeholder is completely dependent on the sustainability of the other two for their own survival.

As a result of this alignment, while other HMOs and IPAs were failing across the country in the 1990s, Kaiser Permanente flourished and grew. By the end of that decade, many of the PMGs had already implemented EHRs with a single medical record for each patient across all specialties. By 2000, they had created population health databases that enabled tracking and management of disease-specific cohorts. On the cost management side, PMGs implemented clinical guidelines with governance structure, policies, and procedures that encouraged consistent improvement in efficiency and effectiveness at every level of service.

There are at least two other positive by-products of the KP model. With mutual exclusivity, 100% of patients in a Permanente physician's practice have the same health insurer, so the administrative environment for clinicians is much less complex than for those contracted with multiple payers. Additionally, all the utilization management and care management functions that are typical of a health plan are delegated to the PMGs. Transferring those resources to the medical group enables those functions to be integrated directly into patient care *and* places them under the direct control of providers.

All that said, the KP model creates its own set of challenges. The single biggest one is that as a closed network, patient choice is limited to Permanente physicians. Anyone switching coverage to Kaiser Health Plan is required to abandon their current providers and choose both their PCP and specialists from within the PMG. This is clearly the most obvious reason that despite its long-term success as an alternative to traditional medical coverage, with membership of 12.6 million Kaiser Permanente remains a relatively small player on the national stage.

There are other, less obvious challenges implied by the KP model that are worth understanding as well. KP struggles with an unusually high overhead for its ambulatory practices with large, owned office buildings that tend to be more expensive than typical private practice office space. Standardized support staff models and investments in governance and management place upward pressure on costs as well.

Another challenge to the KP model is that it is very difficult to replicate. The current PMGs are mature organizations that have been practicing under global capitation for many decades. Even with this long history and mutual exclusivity clauses, the relationship between health plan and providers has been marked by tensions and conflicts that have been manageable only in the context of this long history of codependence.

There are other examples of long-standing payviders, such as the Health Alliance Plan in Michigan and Geisinger in Pennsylvania, but these are relatively small organizations that, from a national perspective, are niche players. In the past decade, however, the health care landscape has begun to change. As providers take on risk and health plans partner with or acquire provider practices, the lines between payer and provider are beginning to blur. Providers and payers that have gained traction in value-based care no longer see each other as opponents in a zero-sum game. While becoming a payvider does not remove tensions between these two functions, it does potentially create a level of interdependence and alignment that can drive efficiency and effectiveness that provides further value for everyone—payer, provider, patients, and the broader community.

Providers have taken various approaches to establishing their health plan capabilities, including attempting to build new expertise internally, through establishing joint ventures or via acquisition. The story of Piedmont WellStar HealthPlans (PWHP) represents a cautionary tale for providers that are pursuing this strategy.[2] In 2013, the Atlanta-based health systems Piedmont Healthcare and WellStar Health System began a joint venture, forming PWHP as a separate legal organization with an independent management team. At launch, PWHP provided coverage for families of all employees of Peidmont and WellStar, about 35,000 people. They also offered a Medicare Advantage plan in specific counties in the Atlanta region.

PWHP entered into management service agreements with several outside organizations, which served as third-party administrators for claims processing, risk management, underwriting, and other payer functions. Just two years later, the joint venture folded, citing costs and headwinds in enrolling Medicare Advantage members. The health plan told providers that the Medicare offering is ending "largely because of an inability to generate a large enough membership and the required premium revenue needed for long-term operations and sustainability. Further, the regulations around [Medicare Advantage] are complex and much more costly to comply with as a small-scale health plan than . . . anticipated."[3] At the time PWHP announced their exit, they had only 12,000 Medicare beneficiaries. Essentially PWHP was unable to achieve adequate membership quickly enough to support a sustainable health plan.

Whereas PWHP involved two provider organizations coming together to form a health plan, Innovation Health is an example of a provider and payer entering into a joint venture. In 2012 in Virginia, Aetna and Inova Health created a joint venture called Innovation Health.[4] Even with the combined assets of Inova's very successful health system in Northern Virginia and Aetna's extensive experience on the payer side, Innovation Health has struggled. In 2015, with a reported membership of 175,000, they announced that they would no longer offer coverage to individuals and families through Virginia's exchange. By 2019, their reported membership was down to 125,000.[5] These numbers suggest that while outperforming the now-defunct PWHP, Innovation Health still faces an uphill battle to become a successful payvider.

Perhaps the most successful example of becoming a payvider lies with United Health Group. With United Healthcare as their flagship health plan, they created Optum Health in 2010 as a subsidiary that, among other things, owns and affiliates with providers. While not technically a payvider, two-thirds of Optum's now $100 billion business is with United Healthcare and they now own or support more than 50,000 providers (and are expecting that number to exceed 60,000 by the end of 2021).[6] They have clearly blurred the line between providers and payers, extracting enormous profits in the process. Efficiencies of scale have driven some benefit to providers, but those enormous profits are essentially extracted from medical cost savings and delivered to their stockholders.

Following in the footsteps of United's success, other major insurers have moved into the provider side of the business as well. In 2018, the merger of Aetna with CVS set the foundation for CVS's MinuteClinics to evolve into the hub of Aetna's provider network. In 2019, Humana announced it is changing its focus from being an insurance company that offers some health care services to becoming a health care provider that also offers insurance.[7] In early 2021, they revealed their plan to transition to 100% ownership of the country's largest home health service, Kindred. Cigna, having acquired Express Scripts in 2019, recently announced the acquisition of a leading national telehealth provider, MDLive.[8]

These tectonic shifts toward vertical integration have huge implications even for those providers that are not considering becoming part of a payvider organization. Providers need to think strategically about their place in the health care ecosystem in a future where competing networks bid for exclusivity with those that demonstrate value and marginalize or exclude those who do not.

Key Takeaways

1. Becoming a payvider is a complex and expensive strategy.
2. Several health plans are moving aggressively into the payvider space.

Recommendations

1. Carefully consider long-term implications for both the practice and the patients served before joining a payer-led payvider system.
2. Focus on adequate scale to become a provider-led payvider system.

PART V

A Shifting Paradigm

CHAPTER 24

Closing Thoughts

This book began with a description of the transition from 4,500 years of gradual and sporadic evolution in our understanding of medical science to a transformational shift in both our understanding and our ability to diagnose and treat in just one century. With that starting point, we have focused on elucidating the parallel transformational shifts in how health care is financed. We have discussed various health plan functions, as well as a range of issues that stand at the interface between providers and payers.

Stepping back from those details, one can appreciate an arc to the history of health care financing in the United States that points toward an uncertain future. The increasing role of government and the evolving strategies of commercial payers set a context for providers that is filled with both risk and opportunity.

In the early 1960s, prior to the introduction of Medicare and Medicaid, 80% of the population was covered by commercial insurance. The 20% left behind were largely composed of the elderly and poor. Considered together, Medicare, Medicaid, military and veteran's benefits, and subsidized exchange products represent the universe of government-sponsored health care that now covers approximately half of all Americans.[1] Within this group, Medicaid leads the way with almost 80 million enrollees and is growing faster than any other segment.

In parallel to this expanding government role is a rapidly transforming dynamic among the large commercial payers. Long gone are the indemnity plans that dominated prior to the 1980s, replaced by an alphabet soup of managed care products. Similarly, the prevalent community-rated insurance of the 1960s has steadily fallen away so that today more than 60% of employer-sponsored coverage is self-insured. The small state and regional health insurers of the 1960s have been replaced by a handful of nationally dominant players. Even within Blue Cross Blue Shield, where there were 67 plans in 1995, today there are only 35, with Anthem alone covering more than 40 million individuals across 14 states.

These "mega" health plans have blurred the lines between payers and providers. United Healthcare, Anthem, CVS/Aetna, Humana, and Cigna have all moved aggressively into the provider arena and now either own or affiliate with providers throughout the country.

Given these dramatic shifts, and the resulting complexity of the payment and regulatory environment, it's not surprising that providers are choosing to be employed as part of a larger group rather than run their practice as a small business. In fact, based on AMA survey results as of 2018, for the first time in history there were fewer physician owners than employees—45.9% versus 47.4%.[2] How far we've come from 1960, when only 8.5% of physicians in the United States were employees.

While the major trends point to greater power for both the government and commercial payers at the expense of providers, the future of health care and how it is paid for, and the position of providers in that dynamic, is not predestined. Today's physicians and other providers are at a crossroads. If they take the short view with a constant focus on how to get through the day and maintain their income, they will likely fall victim to the trends just described. Their nonclinical time and resources will be largely dedicated to incremental adaptations to regulatory changes, payer demands, and shifts in the provider landscape. This path will inevitably lead to continued movement away from independent practice and toward government-funded health care, as well as ever-increasing downward pressure on provider reimbursement.

The alternative path for providers is to shift their paradigm to embrace an uncertain future. Clinician leaders are in a great position to create a vision and strategy that leverages technology to deliver extraordinary service and outcomes to patients, driving value for patients, payers, employers, the community, and, ultimately, themselves. Providers should be leading the work toward prudent adoption of cutting-edge technologies with the goal of creating the most benefit to the most people at the least total cost. Those provider organizations that can demonstrate value will have the government, commercial payers, and consumers at their doorstep. Those clinicians with the courage and vision to pursue an aggressive strategy toward better care for patients, better health outcomes for the community they serve, lower cost trends, and improved provider morale (the Quadruple Aim) will be not victims but architects of the future of health care.

ACRONYMS AND ABBREVIATIONS

ACA	Affordable Care Act
ACE	angiotensin-converting enzyme
ACO	accountable care organization
AHRQ	Agency for Healthcare Research and Quality
AMA	American Medical Association
APC	ambulatory payment classification
APM	alternative payment model
ASO	administrative services only
BMI	body mass index = kg/m^2
CAHPS	Consumer Assessment of Healthcare Providers and Systems
CAT (also CT)	computerized axial tomography
CF	conversion factor
CIN	clinically integrated network
CM	case management
CMS	Centers for Medicare and Medicaid Services
CO-OP	Consumer Operated and Oriented Plan
COPD	chronic obstructive pulmonary disease
COVID-19	coronavirus disease 2019
CPT	current procedural terminology
DRG	diagnosis-related group
ED	emergency department
EDI	electronic data interchange
EHR	electronic health record
EPO	exclusive provider organization

ERISA	Employee Retirement Income Security Act of 1974
FAR	Federal Acquisition Regulation
FFS	fee-for-service
FI	fiscal intermediary
FTE	full-time equivalent
GDP	gross domestic product
HBR	health benefit ratio
HDHP	high-deductible health plan
HIV/AIDS	human immunodeficiency virus / acquired immune deficiency syndrome
HMO	health maintenance organization
HOS	Health Outcomes Survey
HSA	health savings account
IBNR	incurred but not reported
ICD-10	International Statistical Classification of Diseases and Related Health Problems, 10th revision
ICER	Institute for Clinical and Economic Review
IPA	independent physician association
JAMA	*Journal of the American Medical Association*
KFH	Kaiser Foundation Hospitals
KFHP	Kaiser Foundation Health Plan
KP	Kaiser Permanente
KPI	key performance indicator
LOB	line of business
MAC	Medicare administrative contractor
MBR	medical benefit ratio
MCO	managed care organization
MCR	medical cost ratio
MIPS	merit-based incentive payment system
MLR	medical loss ratio
MRI	magnetic resonance imaging
MSO	management services organization
MU	meaningful use
NCQA	National Commission for Quality Assurance
NP	nurse practitioner
OB-GYN	obstetrician-gynecologist or obstetrics and gynecology
P&T	pharmacy and therapeutics

PBM	pharmacy benefit management
PCP	primary care provider
PET	positron-emission tomography
PHM	population health management
PMG	Permanente Medical Group
PMPM	per member per month
POS	point of service
PPO	preferred provider organization
PT	physical therapy
PWHP	Piedmont WellStar HealthPlans
RBRVS	resource-based relative value scale
RCM	revenue cycle management
REACH	Realizing Equity, Access, and Community Health
RN	registered nurse
ROI	return on investment
RUC	Relative Value Scale Update Committee
RVU	relative value unit
SDOH	social determinants of health
SUD	substance use disorder
TPA	third-party administrator
UA	urinalysis
UM	utilization management
VBC	value-based care or value-based contract

NOTES

Chapter 1 • Historical Context

1. Rachel Hajar, "History of Medicine Timeline," *Heart Views* 16, no. 1 (2015): 43–45.

Chapter 2 • What Is a Health Plan?

1. Melissa Thomasson, "Health Insurance in the United States," EH .Net Encyclopedia, ed. Robert Whaples, April 17, 2003. http://eh.net /encyclopedia/health-insurance-in-the-united-states/.

2. Marjorie Smith Mueller, "Health Maintenance Organization Act of 1973," *Social Security Bulletin* 37, no. 3 (March 1974): 35–39. https://www .ssa.gov/policy/docs/ssb/v37n3/v37n3p35.pdf.

Chapter 3 • Medicare

1. "2022 Medicare Parts A & B Premiums and Deductibles/2022 Medicare Part D Income-Related Monthly Adjustment Amounts," Centers for Medicare and Medicaid Services, November 12, 2021, https://www .cms.gov/newsroom/fact-sheets/2022-medicare-parts-b-premiums-and -deductibles2022-medicare-part-d-income-related-monthly-adjustment.

2. "Medicare Administrative Contractors," Centers for Medicare and Medicaid Services, last modified December 1, 2021, https://www.cms.gov /Medicare/Medicare-Contracting/Medicare-Administrative-Contractors /MedicareAdministrativeContractors.

3. "A/B MAC Jurisdictions as of June 2021," accessed August 16, 2022, https://www.cms.gov/files/document/ab-jurisdiction-map-jun -2021.pdf.

4. "Phases of Part D Coverage," Medicare Interactive, August 1, 2022, https://www.medicareinteractive.org/get-answers/medicare -prescription-drug-coverage-part-d/medicare-part-d-costs/phases-of -part-d-coverage.

5. "How to Compare Medigap Policies," Medicare.gov, accessed August 16, 2022, https://www.medicare.gov/supplements-other-insurance /how-to-compare-medigap-policies.

6. "Final Rule: CMS-1717-FC," *Federal Register* 84, no. 218 (November 12, 2019): https://www.cms.gov/files/document/cpi-opps-pa-list -services.pdf.

Chapter 4 • Medicaid

1. Robin Rudowitz, Rachel Garfield, and Elizabeth Hinton, "10 Things to Know about Medicaid: Setting the Facts Straight," Kaiser Family Foundation, March 6, 2019. https://www.kff.org/medicaid/issue-brief/10 -things-to-know-about-medicaid-setting-the-facts-straight/?gclid=CjwKC AiAu8SABhAxEiwAsodSZDSfVShaWYdDqI8bnG8EtztDhDFgpug_H3A 4oZhjc7S9TGoeCkDSMBoCCKEQAvD_BwE.

2. "October and November 2021 Medicaid and CHIP Enrollment Trends Snapshot," November 2021, https://www.medicaid.gov/medicaid /national-medicaid-chip-program-information/downloads/october -november-2021-medicaid-chip-enrollment-trend-snapshot.pdf; "April 2022 Medicaid and CHIP Enrollment Data Highlights," August 1, 2022, https://www.medicaid.gov/medicaid/program-information /medicaid-and-chip-enrollment-data/report-highlights/index.html.

Chapter 5 • Commercial Insurance

1. "Patient Protection and Affordable Care Act; Health Insurance Market Rules; Rate Review," *Federal Register* 78, no. 39 (February 27, 2013): 13408. https://www.federalregister.gov/documents/2013/02 /27/2013-04335/patient-protection-and-affordable-care-act-health -insurance-market-rules-rate-review#h-15.

2. "Market Rating Reforms," Centers for Medicare and Medicaid Services, accessed August 4, 2021. https://www.cms.gov/CCIIO /Programs-and-Initiatives/Health-Insurance-Market-Reforms/Market -Rating-Reforms.

3. P. McDonnell, A. Guttenberg, L. Greenberg, and R. Arnet III, "Self-insured Health Plans," *Health Care Finance Review* 8, no. 2 (Winter 1986): 1–16. https://www.ncbi.nlm.nih.gov/pmc/articles/PMC4191537/.

4. "2021 Employer Health Benefits Survey," November 10, 2021, https://www.kff.org/report-section/ehbs-2021-section-8-high-deductible -health-plans-with-savings-option/.

Chapter 7 • The ABCs of Fee-for-Service
1. W. Hsiao, P. Braiun, D. Dunn, et al., "Resource-Based Relative Values," *Journal of the American Medical Association* 260, no. 16 (October 1988): 2347–53. https://jamanetwork.com/journals/jama/article -abstract/37465.

Chapter 9 • Payment Errors
1. "The Switch from ICD-9 to ICD-10: When and Why," ICD.Codes, October 7, 2015. icd.codes/articles/icd9-to-icd10-explained.
2. "AMA Releases 2022 CPT Code Set," September 7, 2021, https:// www.ama-assn.org/press-center/press-releases/ama-releases-2022-cpt -code-set.
3. "2016 Health Care Cost and Utilization Report—Analytic Methodology," Health Care Cost Institute, January 23, 2018. https://healthcostinsti tute.org/images/pdfs/HCCI_2016_Methodology_v1.0_1.23.18.pdf.

Chapter 10 • Health Plan Strategic Concerns
1. United Health Care, "About Us," accessed August 9, 2021. https:// www.uhc.com/about-us#:~:text=UnitedHealthcare%20is%20dedicated %20to%20helping,working%20lives%20and%20through%20retirement; Anthem Blue Cross and Blue Shield, "About Anthem," accessed August 24, 2022. https://www.anthem.com/about/; Centene, "Our Purpose," accessed August 24, 2022. https://www.centene.com/who-we-are/our-purpose.html; Comparably, "Aetna Mission, Vision & Values," accessed August 9, 2021. https://www.comparably.com/companies/aetna/mission; Cigna, "About Us," accessed August 2021. https://www.cigna.com/about-us/.
2. National Association of Insurance Commissioners, "Medical Loss Ratio," updated July 23, 2021. https://content.naic.org/cipr_topics/topic _medical_loss_ratio.htm#:~:text=The%20ACA%2DMLR%20requires%20 health,administration%2C%20marketing%2C%20and%20profit.

Chapter 11 • Analytics
1. Louise Norris, "CO-OP Health Plans: Patients' Interests First," accessed August 25, 2021. https://www.healthinsurance.org/obamacare /co-op-health-plans-put-patients-interests-first/.

2. Brian Tumulty, "Failure of Health Republic Co-op Part of a Trend," *Democrat and Chronicle*, November 29, 2015. https://www.democrat andchronicle.com/story/news/2015/11/29/health-republic-insurance -affordable-care-act-obamacare/76459200/.

Chapter 12 · Cost Management Strategies

1. "ICER's Impact," accessed August 17, 2022. https://icer.org/who -we-are/history-impact/.

2. Z. Baum, M. Simmons, J. Guardiola, C. Smith, L. Carrasco, J. Ha, and P. Richman, "Potential Impact of Co-payment at Point of Care to Influence Emergency Department Utilization," *PeerJ Life and Environment*, January 21, 2016. https://peerj.com/articles/1544/.

3. V. Ho and M. Heslin, "Effect of Hospital Volume and Experience on In-Hospital Mortality for Pancreaticoduodenectomy," *Annals of Surgery* 237, no. 4 (April 2003): 509–14. https://www.ncbi.nlm.nih.gov/pmc /articles/PMC1514467/.

Chapter 13 · Quality

1. "How to Compare Plans Using the Medicare Star Rating System," Medicare Interactive, accessed August 9, 2021. https://www.medicare interactive.org/get-answers/medicare-health-coverage-options/changing -medicare-coverage/how-to-compare-plans-using-the-medicare-star -rating-system; "Consumer Assessment of Healthcare Providers & Systems (CAHPS)," August 22, 2022, https://www.cms.gov/Research -Statistics-Data-and-Systems/Research/CAHPS; "Health Outcomes Survey (HOS)," accessed August 9, 2021. https://www.cms.gov/Research -Statistics-Data-and-Systems/Research/HOS.

Chapter 14 · Care Management

1. R. Mechanic, "Will Care Management Improve the Value of US Health Care?" Health Industry Forum, 2004. https://heller.brandeis.edu/health -industry-forum/pdfs/background-papers/mechanic-princeton-2004.pdf.

2. R. Goetzel, R. Ozminkowski, V. Vilagra, and J. Duffy, "Return on Investment in Disease Management: A Review," *Health Care Finance Review* 26, no. 4 (Summer 2005): 1–19.

3. S. M. Murphy, J. McGready, M. E. Griswold, and M. L. Sylvia, "A Method for Estimating Cost Savings for Population Health Management Programs. *Health Services Research* 48, no. 2, part 1 (2013): 583. https://doi .org/10.1111/j.1475-6773.2012.01457.x.

4. J. A. West, N. H. Miller, K. M. Parker, D. Senneca, G. Ghandour, M. Clark, G. Greenwald, R. S. Heller, M. B. Fowler, and R. F. DeBusk. "A Comprehensive Management System for Heart Failure Improves Clinical Outcomes and Reduces Medical Resource Utilization." *American Journal of Cardiology* 79 (1997): 58–63.

Chapter 15 • Health Plan Committees
1. "Senate Bill S4611B," 2013–2014 Legislative Session, accessed August 17, 2022. https://www.nysenate.gov/legislation/bills/2013/s4611.

Chapter 17 • Value-Based Budgeting
1. W. Putri, D. J. Muscatello, M. S. Stockwell, and A. T. Newall, "Economic Burden of Seasonal Influenza in the United States," *Vaccine* 36, no. 27 (2018): 3960–66. https://doi.org/10.1016/j.vaccine.2018.05 .057; N. A. Molinari, I. R. Ortega-Sanchez, M. L. Messonnier, W. W. Thompson, P. M. Wortley, E. Weintraub, and C. B. Bridges, "The Annual Impact of Seasonal Influenza in the US: Measuring Disease Burden and Costs," *Vaccine* 25, no. 27 (2007): 5086–96. https://doi.org/10.1016/j .vaccine.2007.03.046.

Chapter 19 • Risk Mitigation
1. G. F. Riley and J. D. Lubitz, "Long-Term Trends in Medicare Payments in the Last Year of Life," *Health Services Research* 45, no. 2 (2010): 565–76. https://doi.org/10.1111/j.1475-6773.2010.01082.x.

2. Ner Tamid Congregation of N. Town v. Krivoruchko, 638 F. Supp. 2d 913 (N.D. Ill. 2009), District Court, N.D. Illinois, Jul 9 2009, II C 2, accessed August 9, 2021. https://www.courtlistener.com/opinion /1490494/ner-tamid-congregation-of-n-town-v-krivoruchko/?q =cites%3A790731.

3. L. Rochefort and R. McRoskey, "The Coronavirus and Force Majeure Clauses in Contracts," Akerman Practice Update, April 6, 2020. https://www.akerman.com/en/perspectives/the-coronavirus-and-force -majeure-clauses-in-contracts.html.

Chapter 20 • Price Transparency
1. "Transparency in Coverage," Federal Register 85 FR 7215 (November 12, 2020), p. 1. Accessed August 25, 2021. https://www .federalregister.gov/documents/2020/11/12/2020-24591/transparency -in-coverage.

Chapter 21 • Subrogation

1. "Subrogation." *Merriam-Webster*, accessed August 9, 2021. https://www.merriam-webster.com/dictionary/subrogation.

2. "Guide to Understanding Subrogation," Phia Group, accessed August 9, 2021, https://www.phiagroup.com/Media/Guide-to-Understanding-Subrogation.

3. "Can Medical or Insurance Providers Claim Rights over Settlement or Judgement Money?" MedWise Insurance Advocacy, accessed August 9, 2021. https://www.medicalinsuranceadvocacy.com/subrogation/.

Chapter 22 • Pharmacy Benefit Management

1. A. Fein, "CVS, Express Scripts, and the Evolution of the PBM Business Model," Drug Channels Institute, May 29, 2019. https://www.drugchannels.net/2019/05/cvs-express-scripts-and-evolution-of.html.

Chapter 23 • On Becoming a Payvider

1. Kaiser Permanente, "Who We Are," accessed August 9, 2021. https://about.kaiserpermanente.org/who-we-are.

2. U. Karkaria, "Piedmont WellStar HealthPlans to Sell Commercial Insurance Oct. 1," *Atlanta Business Chronicle*, August 22, 2013. https://www.bizjournals.com/atlanta/blog/a-healthy-conversation/2013/08/piedmont-wellstar-healthplans-to-sell.html.

3. "Piedmont, WellStar Cutting Back on Health Plan," *Georgia Health News*, September 25, 2015. http://www.georgiahealthnews.com/2015/09/piedmont-wellstar-cutting-health-plan/.

4. Innovation Health, "About Us," accessed August 9, 2021. https://www.innovationhealth.com/en/about-us.html.

5. "Innovation Health Expands Medicare Plans in Northern Virginia," Innovation Health, October 7, 2019. https://www.innovationhealth.com/en/about-us/news-room/expands-medicare-plans-northern-virginia.html.

6. K. Adams, "11 Numbers That Show How Big Optum's Role in Healthcare Is," Becker's Health IT, February 9, 2021. https://www.beckershospitalreview.com/healthcare-information-technology/11-numbers-that-show-how-big-optum-s-role-in-healthcare-is.html#:~:text=Optum%20serves%20more%20than%20125,90%20percent%20of%20U.S.%20hospitals.

7. H. Landi, "Humana's Chief Strategy Officer: Insurance Giant is Shifting to Be a Healthcare Company," Fierce Healthcare, October 3,

2019. https://www.fiercehealthcare.com/payer/humana-strategy-leader
-insurance-giant-shifting-to-be-a-healthcare-company.

8. P. Minemyer, "Cigna's Evernorth Completes Acquisition of Virtual
Care Provider MDLive," Fierce Healthcare, April 19, 2021. https://www
.fiercehealthcare.com/payer/cigna-s-evernorth-completes-acquisition
-virtual-care-provider-mdlive.

Chapter 24 • *Closing Thoughts*

1. R. Cohen, D. Makuc, A. Bernstein, L. Bilheimer, and E. Powell-
Griner, "Health Insurance Coverage Trends, 1959–2007: Estimates from
the National Health Interview Survey," National Health Statistics Report,
No. 17, July 1, 2009. https://www.cdc.gov/nchs/data/nhsr/nhsr017.pdf;
"October and November 2020 Medicaid and CHIP Enrollment Trends
Snapshot," Medicaid and CHIP Learning Collaborative, Centers for
Medicare and Medicaid Services, accessed August 9, 2021. https://www
.medicaid.gov/medicaid/national-medicaid-chip-program-information
/downloads/october-november-medicaid-chip-enrollment-trend-snapshot
.pdf; L. Norris, "Medicare in California," December 10, 2020. https://www
.healthinsurance.org/medicare/california/; K. Schaeffer, "The Changing
Face of America's Veteran Population," Pew Research Center, April 5, 2021.
https://www.pewresearch.org/fact-tank/2021/04/05/the-changing-face-of
-americas-veteran-population/; "Patients by Beneficiary Category," Military
Health System, accessed August 9, 2021. https://www.health.mil/I-Am-A
/Media/Media-Center/Patient-Population-Statistics/Patients-by
-Beneficiary-Category; L. Norris, "Will You Receive an ACA Premium
Subsidy?," HealthInsurance.org, March 11, 2021. https://www.health
insurance.org/obamacare/will-you-receive-an-aca-premium-subsidy/.

2. C. Kane, "Updated Data on Physician Practice Arrangements: For the
First Time, Fewer Physicians Are Owners Than Employees," AMA Economic
and Health Policy Research, May 2019. https://www.ama-assn.org/system
/files/2019-07/prp-fewer-owners-benchmark-survey-2018.pdf.

INDEX

behavioral health care management, 74

benefit design, 61

Blue Cross and Blue Shield, 7, 12, 13, 142

brokers, 28–29

budgeting: and contracts, 96–104; and incentive payments, 107; and pharmacy benefit management, 130–31; and risk, 99, 100, 101, 111–15

"buy-up" programs, 24, 48–49

CAHPS (Consumer Assessment of Healthcare Providers and Systems) scores, 68

capitation. *See* global capitation; partial capitation

care management programs, 29, 48, 49, 50, 56, 72–78

Caremark, 128

carriers, Part B, 12

case management, 62–63

Centers for Medicare and Medicaid Services (CMS): and alternative payment model, 14–16; and attribution logic, 92; Medicare administrative contractors (MACs), 12; and quality ratings, 67–70; reimbursement methodology, 33–35. *See also* Medicaid; Medicare

centers of excellence, 63

certification. *See* credentials

CF. *See* conversion factor

Cigna, 128, 137, 142

CINs (clinically integrated networks), 87

claims: adjudication of, 35, 38–39, 41; audit and recovery, 39–40; claims processing systems, 37, 38, 42–45; and clinical editing software, 39, 40, 41; complexity of, 42–44; consultants' role in, 29–30; filters for, 37, 38; fraud and abuse, 40; and medical policy committees, 81; Medicare Part A/B claims

processing, 12, 13; reimbursement errors, 42–45, 88; reimbursement process, 37–41; and self-insurance, 29–30; as strategic concern, 47

claims processing systems, 37, 38, 42–45

clinical analytics, 56, 58

clinical editing software, 39, 40, 41

clinically integrated networks (CINs), 87

CMS. *See* Centers for Medicare and Medicaid Services (CMS)

codes, payment, 33, 34–35, 39, 42, 43, 106, 120

coinsurance, 13, 15, 35, 61, 119, 120

committees: health plan, 79–83; RUC, 34–35

community fee schedule, 43

community health workers, 74

community rating, 22–23

competition: and pharmacy benefit management, 129; and price transparency, 120; between providers and health plans, 49, 50; and quality ratings, 67–68; as strategic concern, 47, 48

consultants: actuarial, 103, 104; and care management, 76; and contract negotiations, 95; role of, 28–30

Consumer Assessment of Healthcare Providers and Systems (CAHPS) scores, 68

Consumer Operated and Oriented Plan (CO-OP) program, 51, 55

contracts: appendix to, 92; and attribution, 10, 16, 27, 30, 92–93, 97–100; basics, 87–95; and budgeting, 96–104; and claims errors, 88; and claims process, 37, 40; dispute resolution in, 90–91, 95, 100, 114; and duration, 90; financial terms in, 93–94; governance in, 90–91, 95, 114; and incentive payments, 91, 93, 105–10; maturation in, 93; and Medicaid, 19;

Federal Acquisition Regulation (FAR), 12
fee bumps, 105, 107
fee-for-service (FFS): and contract negotiations, 59; and governance, 90–91; and incentive payments, 108; and reimbursement, 33–36
fee schedules and claims processing, 43, 44, 45
filters, claims processing, 37, 38
financial analytics, 55, 57–58
financial terms in contracts, 93–94
fiscal intermediaries, Part A, 12
force majeure clauses, 114–15
fraud and abuse units, 40

gainshare, 91, 109
Geisinger, 135
global capitation, 109
gold carding, 50, 64
governance: committees, 80; in contracts, 90–91, 95, 114
government, role in coverage, 141–43

HDHP. See high-deductible health plans (HDHPs)
Health Alliance Plan, 135
health benefit ratio (HBR). See medical loss ratio (MLR)
health disparities, 61
health literacy, 61, 74
Health Maintenance Organization (HMO) Act, 8
health maintenance organizations. See HMOs (health maintenance organizations)
Health Outcomes Survey (HOS), 68
health plans: analytics, 51–58; and "buy-up" programs, 24, 48–49; committees, 79–83; complexity of, 5–6; consolidation of, 142; defined, 7; strategic concerns of, 46–50, 89; as term, 7. See also claims; contracts; cost control; high-deductible health plans

(HDHPs); insurance, health; insurers, commercial; payviders; reimbursement; self-insurance; value-based contracting
Health Republic Insurance of New York, 55
high-deductible health plans (HDHPs), 5, 25–26, 43, 102
history of medicine, 3–5, 141
HMO-POS. See POS (point of service)
HMOs (health maintenance organizations): and attribution, 92–93, 97; and credentialing, 80; Kaiser Permanente as, 20–21; rise of, 8; and shift to MCOs, 8–9
HOS (Health Outcomes Survey), 68
hospice care, 12, 15
hospitalization, 11–12, 74, 75
Humana, 137, 142

incentive payments, 14, 91, 93, 105–10. See also alternative payment model (APM)
"incurred but not reported" (IBNR) expenses, 55–56
indemnity-based health insurance, 7–8, 9, 22
independent physician associations (IPAs), 33, 87, 109
influenza, 102–3
Innovation Health, 136–37
Inova Health, 136
insurance, health: growth in insured population, 8; vs. health plans, 7; indemnity-based, 7–8, 9, 22; rise of, 7–8; and shift to MCOs, 8–9. See also health plans; Medicaid; Medicare; self-insurance
insurers, commercial: and care management programs, 74, 75–77; complexity of, 20–27; and consultants and brokers, 28–30; funding mechanisms, 22–27; and indemnity-based health insurance, 7–8, 9, 22; and medical loss

ratio, 47; and Medicare Advantage, 12–13; processing of Medicare Part A/B claims by, 12, 13; and quality ratings, 70. *See also* contracts; reimbursement

intensity of services, 60–65

IPAs (independent physician associations), 33, 87, 109

Kaiser Foundation Health Plan, 133

Kaiser Foundation Hospitals, 133

Kaiser Permanente, 20–21, 133–35

Kindred, 137

"look-back" period, 97–98, 99

MACs (Medicare administrative contractors), 12

managed care organizations (MCOs): and credentials, 80–81; vs. health plans, 7; and risk mitigation, 113; shift to, 8–9, 10, 142. *See also* case management; exclusive provider organizations (EPOs); HMOs (health maintenance organizations); PPOs (preferred provider organizations)

management services organizations (MSOs), 48, 49

maturation, in contracts, 93

MDLive, 137

meaningful use (MU), 14

Medicaid: and care management programs, 74–75, 77; and contracts, 93, 96; and cost analytics, 53, 57–58; expansion, 18; federal role in, 17–18; numbers of enrollees, 8, 18–19, 141–42; overview of, 17–19; and quality analytics, 56–57; and quality ratings, 67, 69–70; and risk, 113; states' role in, 17, 69–70

medical cost ratio (MCR). *See* medical loss ratio (MLR)

medical device recalls and subrogation, 125

medical loss ratio (MLR), 47–48, 49

medical policy committees, 81

Medicare: and alternative payment model, 11, 14–16; and care management programs, 74, 75, 77; claims processing for Part A/B, 12, 13; and cost analytics, 57–58; donut hole, 13; financial terms in contracts, 93; influence of, 11, 16; limits on negotiation, 96; and medical loss ratio, 47; Medigap plans, 14, 15; numbers of enrollees, 8, 141–42; overview of, 11–16; parts and products, 11–14; premiums, 12, 13, 51; and quality, 56–57, 67–70; and reimbursement, 14, 33–35; review of plans, 13, 51–52; and risk, 113

Medicare administrative contractors (MACs), 12

Medicare Advantage (Part C): analytics, 51–52; and medical loss ratio, 47; overview of, 12–13; and payviders, 136; and quality, 67–69; review of plans, 13, 51–52; and risk, 113

Medicare and Medicaid Act, 8

Medicare Part A, 11–12, 13, 14, 15

Medicare Part B, 11–12, 13, 14, 15

Medicare Part C. *See* Medicare Advantage (Part C)

Medicare Part D, 12, 13, 14, 47

Medigap plans, 14, 15, 16

merit-based incentive payment system (MIPS), 14

minimum premium arrangements, 25

MinuteClinics, 137

MLR (medical loss ratio), 47–48, 49

MSOs (management services organizations), 48, 49

MU (meaningful use), 14

multispecialty provider groups, 98

narrow networks. *See* tiered networks

National Commission for Quality Assurance (NCQA), 67, 70, 80, 81

negative selection, 52
Nurse Practitioners Modernization Act, 79
nursing facilities, 11, 15

Obamacare. *See* Affordable Care Act (ACA)
OB-GYNs and attribution, 98
Optum Health, 137
Optum Rx, 128

panel size, 88–89
Part A fiscal intermediaries, 12
Part B carriers, 12
partial capitation, 107–10
payment. *See* alternative payment model (APM); incentive payments; reimbursement
payviders, 49, 50, 132–38, 142
PBM (pharmacy benefit management), 29, 48, 49, 127–31
PCPs (primary care providers), 4, 21, 79, 92, 97–98
penalties, late payment, 101
Permanente medical groups, 133
pharmacies, specialty, 129–30
pharmacy and therapeutics (P&T) committees, 82
pharmacy benefit management (PBM), 29, 48, 49, 127–31
Piedmont Healthcare, 136
Piedmont WellStar HealthPlans, 135–37
POS (point of service), 9, 21
PPOs (preferred provider organizations): and attribution, 92–93, 97; and credentials, 80; and MCOs, 9; rise of, 21
preexisting conditions, 22
preliminary reimbursement, 38
premiums: and cost analytics, 52; Medicare, 12, 13, 51; minimum premium arrangements, 25; percent-of-premium arrangements, 93, 96, 112–13; and plan

competition, 48, 59; reviews of, 51, 53; setting, 22–25, 52
prices: and cost control, 59–65; transparency of, 119–22
primary care providers (PCPs), 4, 21, 79, 92, 97–98
prior authorization: and claims processing systems, 38; as form of utilization management, 60–63, 64, 65; and gold/red carding, 50, 64; and health plan committees, 81, 82; and HMOs, 21; and Medicare, 14; and pharmacy benefit management, 129
prior year adjustments, 101
product line exclusions, 10
profit: and analytics, 52–53, 54; and "buy-up" programs, 48, 49; and payviders, 137; providers' focus on, 5; and unattributed members, 98
providers: care management programs by, 49, 50, 77–78; as competing with health plans, 49, 50; decline in ownership by, 142; future paradigms for, 141–43; and health plan committees, 79–83; and indemnity-based health insurance, 8, 9; as payviders, 49, 50, 132–38, 142; profit focus, 5; role in HMOs and MCOs, 9, 21; and self-insurance, 24; shift of administrative functions to, 48, 49; size of, 88–89; strategic position and goals, 88, 89, 111–12; utilization management programs by, 49, 50. *See also* contracts; primary care providers (PCPs); reimbursement
P&T (pharmacy and therapeutics) committees, 82

Quadruple Aim, 143
quality: analytics, 56–57, 58; and attribution, 99, 100; and budgeting, 99, 100, 101; and care